List of titles

OUTLINE STUDIES IN BIOLOGY

Editor's Foreword

The student of biological science in his final years as an undergraduate and his first years as a graduate is expected to gain some familiarity with current research at the frontiers of his discipline. New research work is published in a perplexing diversity of publications and is inevitably concerned with the minutiae of the subject. The sheer number of research journals and papers also causes confusion and difficulties of assimilation. Review articles usually presuppose a background knowledge of the field and are inevitably rather restricted in scope. There is thus a need for short but authoritative introductions to those areas of modern biological research which are either not dealt with in standard introductory textbooks or are not dealt with in sufficient detail to enable the student to go on from them to read scholarly reviews with profit. This series of books is designed to satisfy this need. The authors have been asked to produce a brief outline of their subject assuming that their readers will have read and remembered much of a standard introductory textbook of biology. This outline then sets out to provide by building on this basis, the conceptual framework within which modern research work is progressing and aims to give the reader an indication of the problems, both conceptual and practical, which must be overcome if progress is to be maintained. We hope that students will go on to read the more detailed reviews and articles to which reference is made with a greater insight and understanding of how they fit into the overall scheme of modern research effort and may thus be helped to choose where to make their own contribution to this effort. These books are guidebooks, not textbooks. Modern research pays scant regard for the academic divisions into which biological teaching and introductory textbooks must, to a certain extent, be divided. We have thus concentrated in this series on providing guides to those areas which fall between, or which involve, several different academic disciplines. It is here that the gap between the textbook and the research paper is widest and where the need for guidance is greatest. In so doing we hope to have extended or supplemented but not supplanted main texts, and to have given students assistance in seeing how modern biological research is progressing, while at the same time providing a foundation for self help in the achievement of successful examination results.

J. M. Ashworth, Professor of Biology, University of Essex.

A Biochemical Approach to Nutrition

R.A. Freedland

Professor of Physiological Chemistry
University of California, Davis

and

Stephanie Briggs

Assistant Professor of Nutrition
Kansas State University, Manhattan

LONDON
CHAPMAN AND HALL

A Halsted Press Book
JOHN WILEY & SONS, NEW YORK

First published in 1977
by Chapman and Hall Ltd.
11 New Fetter Lane, London EC4P 4EE
© 1977 R.A. Freedland and Stephanie Briggs
Typeset by Preface Ltd, Salisbury, Wilts, and
printed in Great Britain at the
University Printing House, Cambridge
ISBN 0 412 13040 8

Distributed in the U.S.A.
by Halsted Press, a Division
of John Wiley & Sons, Inc., New York
Library of Congress Cataloging in Publication Data

Freedland, Richard Allan.
    A biochemical approach to nutrition.

    (Outline studies in biology)
    1.   Nutrition.   2.   Biological chemistry.   3.   Meta-
bolism.   I.   Briggs, Stephanie, joint author.   II. Title.
[DNLM: 1.   Nutrition.   2.   Biochemistry,   QU145
F854b]
QP141.F73   612.3   76-45744
ISBN 0-70-98985-8

Contents

Preface

Though the major emphasis of this book will be to provide the nutritionist with a biochemical approach to his experimental and practical problems, it is hoped that the book will also be of use to the biochemist and physiologist to demonstrate how dietary nutrition manipulation can be used as a powerful tool in solving problems in both physiology and biochemistry. There will be no attempt to write an all-encompassing treatise on the relationship between biochemistry and nutrition; rather, it is hoped that the suggestions and partial answers offered here will provide the reader with a basis for approaching problems and designing experiments.

Although some foundation material will be presented in discussions, it is assumed that the reader has a basic knowledge of biochemistry and nutrition and some background in physiology. For supplementary information, references to several basic texts are given at the end of the introduction.

To facilitate easy reference, the book has been divided into chapters according to the roles of the basic nutrients in metabolism. Within chapters, discussion will include such topics as the effects of nutrients on metabolism, the fate of nutrients, the roles of various tissues and interaction of tissues in utilizing nutrients, and the biochemical mechanisms involved.

Toward the end of the book, several example problems will be presented, which we hope will provide the reader with the opportunity to form testable hypotheses and design experiments. The problems will be discussed in the final chapter. We wish to emphasize that the answeres presented are not unequivocal and that the solutions proposed by the reader may be more valid than those offered here.

August 1976   R.A.F.

To my wife, Beverly, and my children, Howard, Judith, and Stephen, whose patience and encouragement were an incentive throughout the writing of this book.

R.A.F.

1 Energy and basal metabolism

It seems appropriate to begin our discussion of nutrients with that concept to which all matter is related; namely, energy. Currently there is a controversy as to whether the kilocalorie or the joule is the proper unit of energy measurement in the metric system. Rather than concerning ourselves with units, we shall simply use the generic term 'energy'. Therefore, what you may have heard referred to as the 'caloric content' of a food shall be referred to here as its 'energy content'.

The energy content of a food stuff can be measured by burning it in a bomb calorimeter. The complete oxidation of the food to carbon dioxide and water (and oxides of other elements, such as nitrogen, contained in the food) transforms the chemical energy of the food to heat, the ultimate form of energy, which can be measured.

Not all the energy in a food stuff is available to the body. Some constituents such as cellulose are not digestible, while others may not be absorbed under all circumstances. That part of a food's energy which can be digested and absorbed is referred to as 'digestible energy'. Not all of the digestible energy is fully oxidized by the body and some must be excreted. For instance, mammals do not completely oxidize nitrogen but excrete it as urea, which still contains extractable energy. Also, in conditions of ketosis that lead to ketonuria, partially oxidized carbon is excreted. The energy in food which can be both absorbed and used by the body is known as 'metabolizable energy'.

When food is metabolized by the body, some of the food's energy is converted to heat, some is used for performing work, and some can be stored. When the energy intake exceeds the body's energy expenditure (work + heat), energy is stored and there is weight gain. When the body's energy expenditure exceeds intake, body substance provides the deficit, and there is weight loss.

'Work' is done not only in the physical sense of force through distance, as during muscular movement, but in a chemical way, through altering bonds. The breaking and forming of chemical bonds is not 100% efficient, and some of the energy inherent in those bonds is lost as heat during conversions. It is for this reason that there is a 'basal metabolic rate', or BMR. BMR is defined as the rate of heat production when the body is in a postabsorptive state and at rest, or that amount of energy required to maintain body function when the body is in a postabsorptive state and at rest. (Rest does not denote sleep; energy expenditure is lower during sleep than during rest.)

As the compounds provided by food are converted via the metabolic pathways to compounds of lower energy levels, some of the energy released in the conversion is trapped in particularly high energy compounds. These high-energy compounds, of which adenosine triphosphate (ATP) is the primary one, can later give up their energy to transform other compounds to higher energy levels, allowing biosynthetic processes and work. Other energy currencies include UTP, GTP, CTP, ITP, and their derivatives.

In many cases it is convenient for the biochemist to account for energy yields as potential ATPs that can be formed from a given food constituent. For certain purposes, counting ATPs has an advantage over using a heat unit such as the kilocalorie or joule, since the amount of metabolic work is directly dependent on ATP (or other high-energy compounds) and not on heat. Examples of work performed by energy transfer from ATP include muscle contraction, maintenance of ion balance, protein synthesis, lipid synthesis and glycogen and lipid storage.

1.1 Turnover of body constituents

It would appear at first glance that an adult animal which had achieved its full growth should require only energy and could accept energy in any available form to maintain bodily functions such as ion balance, respiration, blood flow, and nervous system function. However, even adult animals require protein, minerals, vitamins, and certain fatty acids in addition to energy. This is because the body constituents — proteins, lipids, carbohydrates, nucleic acids, cells — are continually undergoing degradation. Renewal of these constituents requires that substrates for synthesis be continually provided. Hormonal and dietary conditions may alter degradation and synthesis rates, but both processes continue even under extreme conditions. As Schoenheimer discovered in his classic experiments, even when an animal is mobilizing fat stores for energy, some lipid synthesis and fat deposition are occurring [1].

References
[1] Schoenheimer, R. and Rittenberg, D. (1935), *J. biol. Chem.*, **111**, 175.

Recommended Reading
Kleiber, M. (1961), *The Fire of Life.* John Wiley and Sons, Inc., New York.

Schoenheimer, R. (1942), *The Dynamic State of Body Constituents.* Hafner Publishing Co., New York.

General Nutrition Textbooks
Bogert, L. J., Briggs, G. M. and Calloway, D. H. (1973), *Nutrition and Physical Fitness.* W. B. Saunders Co., London.

Pike, R. L. and Brown, M. L. (1975), *Nutrition: An Integrated Approach.* John Wiley & Sons, Inc., London.

Wohl, M. G. and Goodhart, R. S. (1968), *Modern Nutrition in Health and Disease.* Lea & Febiger, Philadelphia.

2 Regulation of enzyme activity

To live in a changing environment requires the ability to adapt. In its day to day existence an animal encounters variation in environmental stresses, in activity requirements, and in type and amount of food intake. To meet an animal's needs in its current situation, the flow of nutrients through its metabolic pathways must be subject to regulation. One of the primary means of controlling the disposition of nutrients is the regulation of enzyme activities.

Enzymes catalyze chemical reactions. The extent to which an enzyme can increase the rate of a reaction depends on the enzyme's activity, which is a function of the amount of active enzyme available and of the presence of substrates, co-factors, inhibitors, and activators. Consequently, enzyme activity is subject to alteration by three basic mechanisms:

1) synthesis and degradation of enzyme molecules;
2) modification of enzyme to an active or inactive form;
3) changes in concentration of substrates, co-factors, activators, or inhibitors.

Each of these mechanisms will be considered individually.

2.1 Enzyme synthesis and degradation

All enzymes are proteins, and therefore enzyme synthesis requires protein synthesis. It appears that in the *in vivo* animal system, protein synthesis is a zero order reaction [1]. This means that a constant amount of enzyme is synthesized per unit time. In contrast, degradation is a first order process [1]: that is, the number of molecules being degraded at any moment is a certain percentage of the number of enzyme molecules present at that moment.

When the rate of synthesis is equal to the rate of degradation, a 'steady state' is said to exist. A change in either synthesis or degradation rate (or both) results in a new steady state, which manifests itself in a change in enzyme activity.

Effecting a change in enzyme activity by this method requires a considerable length of time, normally ten minutes to several days [2,3]. The time required to manifest a change by this mechanism depends upon the degradation rate of the enzyme [3]. Degradation rate is related to another useful concept, the half-life of the enzyme, by the equation,

$$t_{\frac{1}{2}} = \frac{0.693}{d}$$

where $t_{\frac{1}{2}}$ is the half-life (the amount of time required for half the enzyme to disappear when no synthesis is occurring) and d is the degradation rate. The shorter the half-life of the enzyme, the sooner a change in its activity can be manifested following a change in synthesis or degradation rate.

2.2 Conversion to active form

A more rapid mechanism for altering enzyme activity, requiring from a tenth of a second to several minutes, is to convert it from an inactive to an active form, or vice versa. Some such conversions are irreversible, such as the proteolytic activation of trypsinogen to trypsin, chymotrypsinogen to chymotrypsin, and the activation of pepsin. But the reversible conversions, which occur primarily though phosphorylation and dephosphorylation, play a more significant role in the acute regulation of metabolism.

Glycogen synthetase and pyruvic dehydrogenase are examples of enzymes with both phosphorylated and nonphosphorylated forms, the nonphosphorylated form being active [4,5]. In contrast, phosphorylase, an enzyme involved in glycogen breakdown, is active when phosphorylated and inactive when nonphosphorylated [6].

In addition to providing a more rapid means of altering enzyme activity, this mechanism offers a unique potential for amplification of such a change through a series of conversions, as exemplified by the cascade effect in glycogen breakdown. To have a significant effect on glucose-6-phosphate (G6P) production from glycogen, a large portion of the inactive phosphorylase must be activated. However, the signal for 'turning on' the enzyme may be present in only a small quantity and of itself might be insufficient to accomplish the conversion. A single enzyme molecule can catalyze the conversion of many substrate molecules. Therefore, an amplification can be obtained if one enzyme, acting in catalytic amounts, can activate another enzyme, which in turn can activate another enzyme. In the case of glycogen breakdown (Fig. 2.1), a hormone signal triggers the enzyme, adenyl cyclase, at the cellular membrane, catalyzing the formation of cyclic AMP (cAMP) from ATP. Cyclic AMP, known as the 'second messenger' (the first messenger having been the hormone), stimulates the enzyme protein kinase, which catalyzes the conversion of phosphorylase kinase from its inactive to

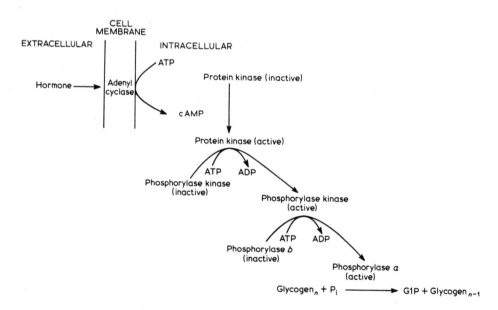

Fig. 2.1 Enzyme cascade for glycogen degradation.

Table 2.1 Magnification of enzyme activity* by cascade mechanism.

Time units passed	Phosphorylase activity†	
	With direct activation	With cascade
1	2500	125 000
2	5000	312 500
3	7500	625 000
4	10 000	1 062 500
5	12 500	1 625 000

*Assume all enzymes have a turnover number of 50 units per unit time (i.e. 50 moles of substrate converted per mole of enzyme per unit time).

†e.g. μmoles G1P produced per unit time.

its active form. Active phosphorylase kinase then catalyzes the phosphorylation of phosphorylase b, making phosphorylase a the active form. Phosphorylase a then acts on glycogen to form glucose-1-phosphate, which eventually can be converted to glucose or used for energy.

Using rather involved calculations, one can determine the degree of magnification of a change in activity after a particular time interval (Table 2.1). Compared to a hypothetical situation in which protein kinase activates phosphorylase directly, the sequential activation results in a significantly greater activity in a given amount of time, whether the activity of the intermediate enzyme is great or small.

2.3 Change in concentrations of metabolic intermediates

Changes in concentrations of substrates, cofactors, activators and inhibitors provide the most acute form of enzyme regulation, with almost immediate manifestations. The velocity of most enzymatic reactions is related to the concentrations of substrates and co-factors by the familiar Michaelis–Menton equation

$$v = \frac{V_m \times (S)}{K_m + (S)}$$

where v is the velocity of the reaction, V_m is the maximal velocity, K_m is the Michaelis constant (i.e. that concentration of substrate at which the velocity is one-half V_m), and (S) is the concentration of substrate (or co-factor).

In the graph of the equation (Fig. 2.2), one can see that the curve is nearly first order in section A and nearly zero-order in section C. This shows velocity to be greatly dependent on substrate concentration when the substrate concentration is low, and almost independent when substrate concentration is high. In section B, the curve is a mixed order function, and, while velocity is still influenced by substrate concentration, a change in substrate concentration would not affect velocity as greatly as would a similar change within section A of the curve. Conditions described by sections A, B, or C of Figure 2.2 are all exemplified in the body by various enzyme reactions. But only when the physiological concentration of substrate occurs at the steep part of the curve can the velocity of the reac-

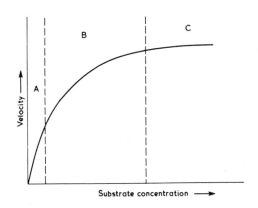

Fig. 2.2 Relation of enzyme activity to substrate concentration.

13

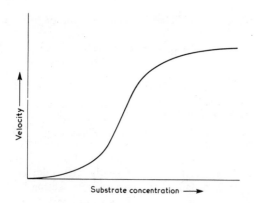

Fig. 2.3 Curve of sigmoidal enzyme kinetics.

tion be regulated by small changes in substrate level.

Physiological concentrations of metabolites are often not in the near-zero range and yet there is regulation of some reactions in which these metabolites participate. These reactions exhibit sigmoidal kinetics. In the sigmoid curve (Fig. 2.3), the steep part occurs at a higher substrate concentration, allowing a small alteration in substrate at that level to cause a large change in velocity of the reaction.

Sigmoidal kinetics are thought to occur as a result of a co-operative binding effect on multiple subunits of an enzyme. In co-operative binding, the first substrate molecule attaches to a subunit with difficulty, but when bound causes a conformation change in the enzyme. This allows subsequent substrate molecules to attach themselves to the other subunits more easily. The greater the concentration of substrate (to a point), the greater the probability that substrate molecules will attach to the other subunits before the original enzyme-substrate complex has formed a product. Consequently, the most rapid change in velocity for a given change in substrate concentration occurs at a higher substrate level.

Either hyperbolic or sigmoid curves can represent the kinetics resulting from activation or inhibition of enzymatic reactions. The effectors can occur naturally in the cell or can come from an exogenous source. An inhibitor may compete with the substrate for the substrate binding requires a higher substrate consubstrate required to maintain a particular velocity. Alternatively, either an inhibitor or an activator can act by attaching to the enzyme at a site different from the substrate-binding site — an 'allosteric' site. The altered conformation of the enzyme resulting from allosteric activation or inhibition can make the formation of the enzyme-substrate complex more easy — in the case of activator, or more difficult — in the case of an inhibitor. Therefore, to achieve the same reaction velocity with an allosteric inhibitor that affects substrate binding, requires a higher substrate concentration than without the inhibitor. That is, the inhibitor has changed the K_m of the substrate for that reaction. Alternatively, the effector may alter the rate of release of the product from the enzyme, thereby changing the maximal rate (V_m) at which the reaction can proceed. Or, an effector may affect both K_m and V_m. Inhibition resulting in increased K_m only is called competitive inhibition and can be overcome by raising substrate concentration. Inhibition which changes V_m only is called noncompetitive and cannot be reversed by increasing the substrate.

As with substrates, the type of curve relating velocity to concentration of allosteric inhibitor or activator depends on the presence or absence of multiple binding sites for the effector. Also as with substrates, the effectiveness of an inhibitor or activator as a regulator of metabolite flow depends on its physiological level relative to the steep part of the kinetic curve.

In addition to providing the possibility for regulation of single reactions, hyperbolic and sigmoidal kinetics can function co-operatively to regulate the disposition of metabolites. Suppose two reactions form products from the same substrate, the first reaction having hyperbolic kinetics and the second having sigmoidal kinetics. The K_m can be low for the first reaction, implying that the velocity relative to V_m will be considerable though the substrate concentration may be low. The K_m for the sigmoid reaction can be much higher and therefore the rate of reaction will be low if the substrate concentration is low. This could be very beneficial if the first reaction were vital to life and the second were a luxury function (for example, fat storage). Should the substrate concentration be low, the luxury function could be sacrificed and the substrate spared for the more vital function. However, if the substrate was increased, both reactions could proceed readily.

References

[1] Schimke, R. T., Sweeney, E. W. and Berlin, C. M. (1965), *J. biol. Chem.*, **240**, 322.

[2] Rechcigl, M. (1971), In *Enzyme Synthesis and Degradation in Mammalian Systems,* **236**. (Ed) Rechcigl, M. University Park Press, Baltimore, Maryland.

[3] Berlin, C. M. and Schimke, R. T. (1965), *Mol. Pharm.*, **1**, 149.

[4] Hers, H. G., DeWulf, H., Stalmans, W. and Van den Berghe, G. (1970, In *Advances in Enzyme Regulation,* **8**, 171. (Ed) Weber, G. Pergamon Press, Oxford.

[5] Wieland, O. H., Siess, E. A., Weiss, L., Loffler, G., Patzelt, C., Portenhauser, R., Hartmann, U. and Schirmann, A. (1973), In *Symposia of the Society for experimental Biology XXVII,* **371**. University Press, Cambridge.

[6] Mayer, S. E. and Krebs, E. G. (1970), *J. biol. Chem.*, **245**, 3153.

Recommended reading

Holzer, H. and Duntze, W. (1972), Chemical modification of enzymes by ATP, pp. 115–136, In *Biochemical Regulatory Mechanisms in Eukaryotic Cells.* (Eds) Kun, E. and Grisolia, S. John Wiley & Sons, Inc., New York.

Atkinson, D. E. (1966), Regulation of enzyme activity, pp. 85–124, In *Annual Review of Biochemistry,* **35** (I). (Eds) Boyer, P. D., Meister, A., Sinsheimer, R. L. and Snell, E. E. Annual Reviews, Inc., Palo Alto, California.

Rechcigl, M., ed. (1971), *Enzyme Synthesis and Degradation in Mammalian Systems.* University Park Press, Baltimore, Maryland.

Newsholme, E. A. and Start, C. (1973), *Regulation in Metabolism.* John Wiley and Sons, Ltd., London.

3 Carbohydrates

3.1 Structure and role

Carbohydrates constitute the greatest portion of the food consumed in the world, by man and animals. The most commonly found forms of carbohydrate are cellulose and starches; polymeric chains of glucose which serve as the structural and energy storage components of plants, respectively.

The glucose units of cellulose are bonded together linearly in $\beta1-4$ linkage, a bond which can be enzymatically broken only by micro-oranisms. The energy of cellulose therefore is available to an animal only to the extent that its digestive tract contains micro-organisms with the enzyme to break this bond. Man is unable to digest cellulose, whereas the cow, which has a rumen with a large microflora population, is able to obtain a large portion of its energy indirectly from cellulose.

The starches — amylose, a linear chain with $\alpha,1-4$ glycosidic linkage, and amylopectin, a branched chain with both $\alpha,1-4$ and $\alpha,1-6$ glycosidic bonds — can be digested by higher animals. Another starch, glycogen, though not a quantitatively important food substance, is also digestible by higher animals. Known as 'animal starch', glycogen resembles amylopectin but has a higher percentage of 1—6 linkages.

Other dietarily important carbohydrates include the disaccharides, sucrose and lactose. Sucrose contains a molecule of glucose and one of fructose, connected in $\beta,1-2$ linkage. Lactose, or 'milk sugar', is the union fo glucose and galactose in $\beta,1-4$ linkage. Both disaccharides are split by specific gut enzymes, sucrase and lactase, into their monosaccharide moieties before any absorption takes place.

In addition to serving as an energy source for animals, carbohydrate can be stored in small amounts as glycogen, providing a glucose reserve. Though not substantial for long-term stress or deprivation, glycogen breakdown can provide energy and maintain blood glucose in acutely stressful situations. Carbohydrate can also play a structural role, as in chondroitin sulphate, a component of cartilage, and in chitin, a constituent of the hard outer shell of insects and crustaceans. Metabolically, carbohydrates are also an important precursor of lipids, forming both the fatty acid and glycerol moieties. In addition, carbohydrates can provide the carbon skeleton for the non-essential amino acids.

In spite of these many roles of carbohydrate, there appears to be no 'essential' dietary carbohydrate (except for vitamin C in some species). Glucose and the other carbohydrate structures found in the body can all be synthesized from non-carbohydrate precursors. However, though rats fed carbohydrate-free diets containing adequate protein can gain weight, they do not gain as fast as those consuming diets containing carbohydrates [1]. It has also been found that chickens eating diets high in free fatty acids require some carbohydrate to maintain growth [2]. In man, there is some evidence that dietary carbohydrate aids digestion and absorption. Current investigation indicates even that non-digestible matter, such as cellulose and pectin, may be important for maintaining optimal gut motility [3].

Glucose is a very important fuel in the body — the only fuel acceptable to the red blood cell and the kidney medulla. The central nervous system, including the brain, is not entirely dependent on glucose, being able to burn ketone bodies, but it has a definite requirement for glucose [4]. Under anaerobic conditions, glucose is the only potential energy source, but when oxygen is present some tissues (e.g. skeletal muscle, heart) can use other fuels, such as fatty acids and ketone bodies. Adipose tissue needs glucose to make the α-glycerol phosphate moiety (αGP) required for triglyceride formation. The liver is exceptional in that it is not a good glucose burner. It is enzymatically better suited to the production of glucose, and oxidizes fatty acids in preference to this.

Since some tissues of the body have an absolute requirement for glucose, maintenance of adequate glucose levels in the blood for distribution to these systems is of first-order importance. Consequently, it is not surprising to find a complex set of metabolic controls for the disposition of glucose. The remainder of this chapter will be devoted to a detailed study of the control points of glucose metabolism and to the development of an appreciation of the adaptations made to varying dietary and hormonal conditions.

3.2 Regulation of glucose metabolism: formation of G6P

Briefly outlined, the disposition of glucose follows this pattern: When dietary glucose is in abundance, the glucose level of the blood entering the liver is high. Some glucose is stored in the liver as glycogen and some is converted to fatty acids. The still high blood glucose circulates to the periphery where it provides fuel for those systems enzymatically equipped to burn it. In muscle, some of the glucose may be used to provide ATP, some will be stored as glycogen and some will be used in biosynthetic processes. In adipose tissues, glucose can make αGP, and

depending on the species of animal, fatty acids, resulting in the storage of fat. In general, when glucose is abundant and other essential nutrients are adequate, systems are geared to anabolic processes and storage.

When glucose is in short supply, glucose stores in the liver are mobilized to maintain the blood glucose level, fat stores are mobilized to provide alternative energy sources so sparing glucose reserves, and the synthesis of glucose by liver and kidney from non-carbohydrate precursors is stimulated. When glucose is low, as in starvation, systems are working to maintain blood glucose and to conserve it by providing alternate fuel sources.

The first step in the utilization of glucose by many tissues requires the presence of the pancreatic hormone insulin. When blood glucose becomes elevated, the normal pancreas is stimulated to secrete insulin. Insulin then circulates to the periphery, where it increases the permeability of cell membranes to glucose. (Entry of glucose into liver and brain appears not to be insulin dependent.) In the absence of insulin, as in the untreated diabetic, glucose can enter the cells by passive diffusion, but does so at a very slow rate, with the effect that the cells appear to starve while bathed in glucose. Insulin, which is destroyed primarily by the liver, has a short half-life, approximately 20 minutes [5]. Consequently, insulin's activity will remain high only as long as the glucose level of the blood is high enough to stimulate insulin secretion by the pancreas.

With this interdependency of glucose and insulin levels, it is not always possible to separate the effects of glucose from those of glucose plus insulin, particularly in the whole animal. Insulin itself is thought to have direct metabolic effects, i.e. on protein synthesis. In the present discussion, no attempt will be made to distinguish between the effects of glucose and of glucose plus insulin unless well-documented distinctions are known.

Once it has entered the cell, glucose can be phosphorylated by hexokinase to become glucose-6-phosphate (G6P). As with most phosphorylated intermediates, G6P cannot cross the cell membrane and is therefore destined to follow one of several paths: the glycolytic pathway, the hexose-monophosphate (HMP) pathway, the glycogen synthesis pathway, or if in liver, possible reconversion to glucose. Being a physiologically irreversible reaction, glucose→ G6P is a reaction likely to be subject to regulation.

Hexokinase, which occurs in many tissues, is a 'constitutive' enzyme (i.e. one whose activity does not change greatly with nutritional and hormonal variation) and has a low K_m for glucose, about $10 \mu M$. An ordinary blood glucose level, such as 90 mg/100 ml, or 5 mM, is well above the K_m of hexokinase. Consequently, in liver cells, where glucose concentration is the same as that of blood, hexokinase is always near zero-order kinetics (i.e. near V_m), producing G6P at a nearly constant rate regardless of increases in glucose concentration. Were hexokinase permitted to form G6P as long as blood glucose is available, blood glucose could be reduced to levels below $10 \mu M$, too low to sustain life.

The form of control imposed on hexokinase is a negative feedback mechanism: allosteric inhibition of the enzyme by the reaction's product, G6P. Negative feedback is particularly appropriate here since G6P concentration is the primary marker indicating the flooding of the branching pathways. G6P inhibits hexokinase by changing V_m (non-competitive inhibition) [6]. Lowering V_m is more effective than changing K_m in this situation, since ordinary glucose levels are about 500 times the K_m of hexokinase for glucose. In order for a change in K_m to be significant, it would have to be of considerable magnitude, about 100-fold, whereas most of the K_m changes reported for other enzymes are less than 10-fold.

The inhibition of hexokinase by G6P has been reported to be as high as 95% in muscle [6]. Since hexokinase provides the only means for utilizing glucose in muscle, the build-up of G6P due to saturation of glycogen synthesis, HMP, and glycolysis limits the removal of glucose from the blood by muscle.

In liver, however, hexokinase activity is low and is greatly exceeded by the activity of glucokinase, another enzyme which phosphorylates glucose. Glucokinase is adaptive (i.e. can increase in quantity with dietary or hormonal stimuli) and has a K_m of about 10mM, very near the normal blood glucose range of 5 to 10 mM. Glucokinase is not inhibited by G6P and can continue to phosphorylate glucose as long as the glucose concentration remains high. Because of the high K_m, there is no threat of reducing blood glucose to dangerously low levels.

The build-up of G6P in liver when blood glucose is high can stimulate glycogen formation and also the reconversion of G6P to glucose by G6Pase, an enzyme unique to liver and kidney cortex. The formation of G6P from glucose, which requires ATP, and the reconversion of G6P to glucose and inorganic phosphate (P_i) could be regarded as wasteful of energy — a 'futile' cycle (also known as a 'substrate' cycle). But such a cycle, though costing energy, enables the liver simultaneously to maintain the capacity to remove glucose from the blood and to add glucose back to the blood. The direction of net flux of glucose between liver and blood appears to be simply a matter of the amounts of glucokinase and G6Pase and the availability of their substrates. When blood glucose is low, the pancreas releases a hormone, glucagon, which stimulates the rapid breakdown of liver glycogen. The resultant increase of intracellular G6P and the low blood glucose level lead to a net flux of glucose from the liver into the blood.

Glycogen in muscle can also be converted

to blood glucose, but not directly since muscle has no G6Pase. Rather, the muscle can burn the glucose units of glycogen to lactate, for which it gains three high energy phosphates per glucose unit, and can release the lactate into the blood. Circulating to the liver, the lactate can be removed and reconverted to glucose by gluconeogenesis, a process limited to liver and kidney cortex. The glucose thus formed can return via the bloodstream to muscle. The Cori cycle, as this is called, provides the muscle with energy under anaerobic conditions without sacrificing the glucose forming potential of its glycogen. However, as with all synthetic processes, it is not without cost. Formation of one glucose from two lactate units requires an input of 6 ATPs. Thus, there is a net expenditure of 3 high energy phosphates per glucose formed from muscle glycogen.

There is no energy loss in converting liver glycogen to glucose (although production of glycogen requires two ATPs per glucosyl unit, in liver and in muscle). Consequently, the liver appears to be the more advantageous site for the storage of greater amounts of glycogen for purposes of maintaining blood glucose. The glucokinase by-pass, which allows continued phosphorylation of glucose even after the inhibition of hexokinase and creates the increased G6P concentrations necessary to increase glycogen formation in liver, would seem to be judiciously placed.

So far, we have discussed the regulation of the formation of G6P, an intermediate which can then proceed along one of several pathways. Conceivably, the flux through any of these pathways could be determined merely by substrate (G6P) availability and the activity potential of the most limiting enzyme. In the cases of glycogen formation and for some tissues, glycolysis, (HMP will be discussed in the chapter on lipids) the situation is more complicated. These two pathways can run in both forward

and reverse directions: glycogen synthesis or glycogen degradation, glycolysis or gluconeogenesis. The direction of flux, a matter of great importance for the well-being of the animal, is regulated — often by more than one mechanism. Regulation occurs at the non-equilibrium reactions, which, to be reversible, must be catalyzed in opposite directions by separate enzymes.

3.3 Glycogen metabolism

In glycogen metabolism, the regulated enzymes are glycogen synthetase (UDP–glucose + glycogen$_{n-1}$ → glycogen$_n$ + UDP) and phosphorylase (glycogen$_{n+1}$ + P$_i$ → glycogen$_n$ + G1P). (See the phosphorylase cascade presented in Chapter 2.) Both enzymes occur in active and inactive forms. When glycogen synthetase is phosphorylated, it is inactive; when phosphorylase is phosphorylated it is active. Protein kinase, one of the enzymes in the cascade for activation of phosphorylase, also inactivates glycogen synthetase. This action of protein kinase guarantees that while phosphorylase is predominantly active, glycogen synthetase will be predominantly inactive. Energy loss through substrate cycling is thereby minimized, and the use of G6P from glycogen for blood glucose maintenance or immediate tissue energy needs is not hampered by the reforming of glycogen.

Glycogen synthetase can also be activated by high concentrations of G6P. A high level of G6P is unlikely to occur in muscle because of the negative feedback inhibition on hexokinase. In liver, however, because of glucokinase and in spite of G6Pase, G6P can build up after a high carbohydrate meal [7]. The resulting stimulation of glycogen synthetase then allows for the storage of extra carbohydrate. Insulin too, which would be high after a large carbohydrate meal, can activate glycogen synthetase and may also inactivate phosphorylase [8]. The mechanisms by which insulin affects glycogen synthesis are not well understood.

The breakdown of glycogen is often a

response to an emergency situation: in the case of liver glycogen, a response to an internal emergency of low blood glucose, and in the case of muscle, to an external threat requiring the immediate availability of fuel for muscle movement. The cascade for glycogen breakdown in such situations is triggered by hormonal messengers; glucagon in the liver and epinephrine (adrenaline) in the muscle. Low blood glucose stimulates the secretion of glucagon, and stressful situations (fear, extreme tension, exercise) cause the release of epinephrine. The entire tissue responds to the hormonal message. In liver, glucagon is the physiological trigger of glycogen breakdown. In muscle, glycogenolysis can be activated by two mechanisms in addition to epinephrine. These mechanisms operate at a more localized level.

Muscle contraction is accompanied by a release of Ca^{++} from vesicles of the sarcoplasmic reticulum. Ca^{++}, at levels measured in muscle tissue during contraction, have been found to activate phosphorylase b kinase [9]. By-passing the first half of the cascade system, the Ca^{++} activation of glycogenolysis is a local response to activity of a particular muscle. This can be advantageous when a single set of muscles is in use and there is no need for movement or readiness in all muscles.

On a cellular level, muscle glycogenolysis can be stimulated by high levels of $5'$-AMP. If the cascade is entirely by-passed, AMP can activate phosphorylase b. The high AMP can be reduced (and ATP increased) by glycolysis following formation of G6P from glycogen.

A suitable mechanism in muscle, AMP activation of phosphorylase b would not be an advantage in liver and does not occur there. If a liver cell were to have a low energy level, the energy deficit would not be overcome by breakdown of glycogen since the liver does not readily oxidize G6P but rather converts it to glucose.

3.4 Glycolysis

The conversion of G6P to pyruvate (or lactate) is for muscle an energy-producing process, and, not surprisingly, the main regulator determining the flux through this pathway is the energy status indicator, ATP. Phosphofructokinase (PFK), the enzyme catalyzing the first non-equilibrium reaction unique to glycolysis (F6P + ATP → FDP + ADP), requires ATP as a substrate but also shows inhibition by high levels of ATP. The ATP inhibition of PFK is enhanced by citrate, a compound which increases greatly in muscle when fatty acids or ketone bodies are being utilized for energy [10]. By this mechanism, when alternate fuel sources are available, carbohydrate is conserved, since inhibition of PFK leads to an increase in fructose-6-phosphate (F6P) concentration, which causes, through equilibrium, an increase in G6P and a consequent inhibition of hexokinase (Fig. 3.1).

This control mechanism is also responsible for an apparent anomaly − the increase in glycogen content of the heart during starvation. The heart, being amply supplied with oxygen, readily burns fatty acids and ketone bodies, which are elevated during starvation. The resulting high levels of ATP, and particularly citrate, strongly inhibit PFK. Therefore, glucose which enters the heart and is phosphorylated (although hexokinase would be inhibited, it is not 100% shut off), is largely prevented from traversing glycolysis. Consequently, concentrations of F6P and G6P are increased. In addition, the elevated ATP levels (thus low AMP levels) prevent phosphorylase from manifesting its full activity, while the high G6P serves both as activator of glycogen synthetase and precursor of UDPG via G1P. These conditions lead to a slow but constant accumulation of glycogen, an unexpected phenomenon during starvation but one that is consistent with the recognized biochemical controls.

where on fig 2.1

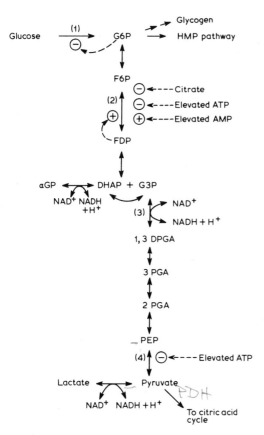

Fig. 3.1 Regulation of glycolysis. Numbers indicate regulated steps and dotted lines indicate stimulatory or inhibitory effects. (1) Hexokinase is inhibited by high levels of G6P, thereby preventing excessive accumulation of G6P and glucose depletion. (2) Phosphofructokinase is inhibited by high levels of ATP and citrate as well as by elevated ATP/AMP. A major purpose of glycolysis is to produce ATP, and a signal of high ATP will decrease glycolysis. This will conserve glucose and increase glycogen. (3) If NAD^+ is not available, G3P cannot be oxidized. Therefore, it is important for the cell to re-oxidize the NADH to NAD by one of three major procedures: (a) by moving the reducing power into the mitochondria (see Fig. 5.2) and through the electron transport chain. This requires aerobic conditions; (b) by converting the pyruvate formed into lactate. This can be accomplished anaerobically; (c) by conversion of DHAP to α-glycerol phosphate. This may be limited by high α-GP concentrations, which, unlike lactate, will not leave the cell. (4) Pyruvate kinase is the last physiologically unidirectional enzyme of glycolysis and is inhibited by elevated ATP levels, permitting an upward flow to α-GP or glycogen when the energy charge is high.

The ATP inhibition of PFK can be overcome by high levels of F6P. High F6P is not likely to occur in muscle from blood glucose sources because of the hexokinase inhibition, but during glycogen breakdown resulting from a hormonal stimulus, F6P could conceivably build up to high enough levels to override the ATP inhibition. High AMP, the signal of a low energy status is also effective in overcoming the ATP inhibition of PFK.

In liver and kidney, PFK is subject to the same regulators as in muscle. But an added aspect to the system is the reverse reaction FDP → F6P + P_i, catalyzed by fructose diphosphatase (FDPase). FDPase occurs in muscle but at such low activity as not to be a significant regulator of flux through glycolysis. In the gluconeogenic tissues its activity is significant — in fact, greater than the activity of PFK. There is evidence of the occurrence of substrate cycling between PFK and FDPase, with the net flux in liver and kidney being toward glucose [11]. The two enzymes are oppositely affected by AMP. In a situation such as anoxia, the removal of inhibition from PFK due to the resulting low ATP/high AMP

21

and the inhibition of FDPase by high AMP can reverse the direction of flux in the liver to favor formation of lactate.

3.5 Pyruvate metabolism

The remaining reactions of glycolysis, to the formation of pyruvate or lactate, with the exception of pyruvate kinase, are non-regulated equilibrium reactions. The disposition of pyruvate, however, is regulated with great advantage to the animal system. In muscle, pyruvate can form either lactate or acetyl CoA. In the central nervous system, adipose tissue, and liver and kidney, pyruvate has the added possibility of combining with CO_2 to form oxaloacetic acid (OAA). Lactate, pyruvate, and OAA can serve as substrates for glucose formation in liver and kidney and for glycolytic intermediates such as dihydroxyacetonephosphate (DHAP) in adipose tissue. However, once pyruvate has been converted to acetyl CoA, its glucose-forming potential is lost. There can be no net glucose production from acetyl CoA because it is a two-carbon compound and two carbons are lost as CO_2 shortly after acetyl CoA enters the citric acid cycle. Therefore, regulation of pyruvate dehydrogenase (PDH), a mitochondrial enzyme which catalyzes the unidirectional reaction

$$pyr + CoA + NAD \rightarrow Acetyl\ CoA + NADH + CO_2$$

offers protection of glucose-producing potential.

In keeping with its critical position in the pathway, PDH is regulated by several mechanisms. One mechanism is negative feedback: inhibition by acetyl CoA and NADH, both of which are products of the reaction [12]. This is fitting because the main purpose of the citric acid cycle, which acetyl CoA enters, is to produce energy by forming NADH and $FADH_2$, which can then be oxidized in the electron transport chain to yield ATP. (A

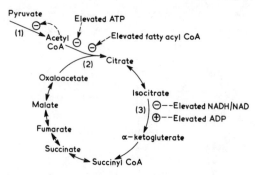

Fig. 3.2 Regulation of the citric acid cycle. (1) Pyruvic dehydrogenase, in addition to having an active and an inactive form, is also inhibited by elevated acetyl CoA levels. (2) Citrate synthetase is inhibited by elevated ATP and/or elevated long chain fatty acyl CoA. This allows acetyl CoA to accumulate and conserves pyruvate as a glucogenic precursor. (3) The NAD^+-linked isocitrate dehydrogenase is inhibited by elevated NADH/NAD, which can occur when there is insufficient ADP to couple electron transport for ATP formation. The elevated citrate can enter the cytoplasm where it can help inhibit glycolysis or, in certain tissues, become a precursor for fatty acid synthesis.

scheme of the regulation of the citric acid cycle is shown in Fig. 3.2). If the NADH level is already high, there is no need to make more, and the glucose potential of pyruvate can be conserved. Also, if the acetyl CoA concentration is high, there is no need to convert more pyruvate to acetyl CoA.

Pyruvate dehydrogenase also occurs in active and inactive forms. The inactivation of PDH (by phosphorylation) is inhibited by ADP and pyruvate, additively [13]. This benefits the animal in that, when energy is low (high ADP), PDH can remain active to provide acetyl CoA for the citric acid cycle, ultimately yielding ATP. Likewise, when pyruvate is abundant, even though ADP may be low (i.e. ATP high), the pyruvate can be used to generate acetyl CoA, a potential precursor of fatty acids.

When PDH is in the inactive form, it is activated by a phosphatase that requires either Mg^{++} or Ca^{++} as a co-factor [14]. Certain naturally occurring compounds, namely citrate and ATP, can chelate these divalent cations, making them unavailable as co-factors for the phosphatase and thereby inhibiting the activation of PDH. When citrate and/or ATP are high, the citric acid cycle has been well provided for and needs no products from PDH.

The nutritional and hormonal state of the animal determines the proportion of this enzyme that is in the active form. The proportion varies also from tissue to tissue, depending on the function of the enzyme in the tissue. Table 3.1 shows the percentage of PDH that is in the active form in several tissues, both in the fed and in the starved states. The observed decrease in the percentage of active PDH in heart and kidney after 24 hours of starvation is consistent with the ability of these tissues to utilize fatty acids and ketone bodies. The brain however, which is still heavily dependent on glucose during the early stages of starvation, shows little change in the

percentage of active PDH. In both liver and adipose, there is a very low proportion of the enzyme in the active form even during the fed state, indicating that these two tissues do not burn pyruvate at a near maximal rate, as do heart and brain. Furthermore, they show a decrease with starvation [13]. When the liver produces ketone bodies, it depends primarily on fatty acids for energy.

When starved animals are re-fed various substances, the effects on the proportion of active PDH are consistent with the previously explained control theories. In all the following examples, animals were fed and then killed 3 hours later for analysis of heart PDH [15]. If no substance was fed, only 3% of the enzyme remained in the active form. If olive oil was eaten, there was no change from the starvation state. This would be expected because olive oil produces no carbohydrate and offers no change in fuel for the starved animal. However, if glucose was consumed, 75% of the enzyme was found in the active form after 3 hours. If fructose was fed, 50% of the enzyme was found in the active form. In brief, a carbohydrate load provided a new fuel and created the need for increased PDH activity.

Along with ingestion of glucose there is an accompanying insulin release. It has been observed in diabetic animals that only 6% of the PDH in heart and 8% of the PDH in kidney are in the active form. After administration of insulin, the percentages increase to 30 in heart and 40 in kidney. Insulin, in addition to increasing cellular uptake of glucose, causes a decrease in circulating non-esterified fatty acids. If one plots the percentage of PDH in the active form versus the concentration of non-esterified fatty acids, an inverse relationship is observed [13, 16]. It has been further observed that there is a strong negative correlation between the concentration of fatty acyl CoA and the percentage of active PDH in many cells. However, it is uncertain as to

Table 3.1 Effects of dietary and hormonal treatments on the relative proportion of pyruvic dehydrogenase in the active form.*

Tissue	Percentage of pyruvic dehydrogenase in the active form	
	Fed	Starved
Heart	75	14
Kidney	75	14
Brain	75	75
Liver	20	10
Adipose	20	7

*Taken from papers and talks of O. Wieland [13–16]

whether an increase in fatty acyl CoA is directly responsible for the inactivation of PDH or whether the inactivation is mediated by an increase in the mitochondrial ATP/ADP ratio, which is also negatively correlated with PDH activity and which accompanies any increase in fatty acyl CoA [13–16].

When fatty acids or lipids are consumed in the absence of a carbohydrate, insulin levels remain low. If an animal is given a strictly lipid diet, though it is not starving, its metabolic responses are similar to those observed in starvation, as exemplified above with PDH. High levels of non-esterified fatty acids and low insulin are indicators that an animal is in the starving state, whereas elevated glucose and insulin levels signal the fed state. These indicators of the fed or starving state are, directly or indirectly, the signals to convert PDH to its active or inactive form.

By converting PDH to its inactive form during starvation, the animal system protects the glucose-forming potential of available carbohydrate. If pyruvate were not conserved, the entire glucose requirement would have to be met by body protein and glycerol, the only other sources of substrate for gluconeogenesis. Thus, by conserving pyruvate, the animal indirectly conserves its body protein.

3.6 Gluconeogenesis

Two enzymes intimately involved in gluconeogenesis are pyruvate carboxylase and phosphoenolpyruvate carboxykinase (PEPCK; also known as phosphoenolpyruvate carboxylase). Their two reactions are required for gluconeogenesis to circumvent the pyruvate kinase reaction (PEP + ADP → pyruvate + ATP), which under physiological conditions is unidirectional. Although having a wide tissue distribution, these two enzymes are the most active in the glucogenic tissues, liver and kidney cortex. As could be expected from their functions, pyruvate carboxylase and PEPCK

are subject to regulation and their activities can vary greatly with nutritional and hormonal conditions.

Under nutritional conditions where gluconeogenesis would be important – high protein or high lipid diets with low carbohydrate, or starvation – there appears to be no change in the total potential activity of pyruvate carboxylase. However, there are some strong allosteric effectors of pyruvate carboxylase favoring the formation of OAA from pyruvate. ATP, which is also a required co-factor, is an allosteric activator, while ADP is an inhibitor. Acetyl CoA positively affects pyruvate carboxylase and shows sigmoidal kinetics [17]. The ordinary concentration of acetyl CoA in liver is near the concentration required to activate the enzyme half-maximally, near the point of greatest inflection of the sigmoid curve. Thus, small changes in the level of acetyl CoA can markedly affect the activity of the enzyme.

These effectors, ATP/ADP and acetyl CoA, affect pyruvate carboxylase and pyruvate dehydrogenase oppositely. Thus, the increased fatty acid metabolism in liver associated with starvation or high lipid diets has two major effects. The product of β-oxidation, namely acetyl CoA, inhibits PDH and activates pyru-

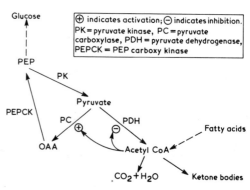

Fig. 3.3 Regulation of pyruvate metabolism.

vate carboxylase. Thus, in situations where there is a shortage of carbohydrate, pyruvate is shunted toward the gluconeogenic pathway (see Fig. 3.3).

PEPcarboxykinase appears to be controlled primarily by increasing and decreasing the total amount and potential activity of the enzyme, although undiscovered allosteric effectors may play a role. With starvation, high protein diet or high lipid diet, the activity of PEPCK rises markedly [18]. Activity diminishes rapidly after ingestion of a high carbohydrate diet [19]. This allows greater gluconeogenesis when glucose is in short supply and reduces the process when glucose supply is adequate.

The subcellular distribution of PEPCK varies among species [20]. In the rat it appears to be strictly a cytoplasmic enzyme, whereas in guinea pig and rabbit it is found both in cytoplasm and mitochondria. In birds it occurs only in mitochondria. Where PEPCK is strictly mitochondrial, the PEP formed in the mitochondria is able to pass across the mitochondrial membrane into the cytoplasm where it can be converted to glucose. This is exceptional since in most mammalian systems phosphorylated intermediates do not readily cross membranes and are trapped in the compartment where they are synthesized. In the rat, the four-carbon compound formed by pyruvate carboxylase must return to the cytoplasm for the PEPCK reaction. However, oxaloacetate does not readily cross the mitochondrial membrane in rat liver or kidney and must be converted to aspartate or malate before transfer. In species where PEPCK occurs in both compartments, theories as to which one plays the greater role in gluconeogenesis are in conflict. However, the activity of the cytoplasmic enzyme is altered by nutritional and hormonal changes that cause increased gluconeogenesis, whereas the mitochondrial one is not [21]. Thus, the cytoplas-

mic enzyme appears to be the more important in gluconeogenesis [22, 23].

The co-ordination of PDH, pyruvate carboxylase, and PEPCK has been demonstrated in many experiments, both with perfused liver and in whole animals. Perfusion of liver with butyrate or oleate (acetyl CoA precursors) causes marked increases in gluconeogenesis from compounds which must pass through pyruvate to be converted to glucose, such as pyruvate itself, lactate, and alanine [24]. Furthermore, a lower percentage of the pyruvate (or other precursor) present is converted to acetyl CoA. Even in dairy cows, which are more dependent on continual gluconeogenesis that are non-ruminants, butyrate increases the proportion of pyruvate entering the gluconeogenic pathway [25].

3.7 Galactose and fructose metabolism

It has been our intention throughout this discussion to emphasize the systems for regulation of carbohydrate flow in the living animal and to show how regulation permits the animal to adapt to changing dietary intakes. We would now like to point out two situations in which the control systems appear at times to be inadequate in directing incoming carbohydrate, to the detriment of the body. These concern the two dietary disaccharides that contain non-glucose moieties: lactose, containing galactose, and sucrose, containing fructose.

Galactose is normally metabolized as outlined in Fig. 3.4. This conversion takes place primarily in the liver, where the enzyme galactokinase occurs in highest concentration. However, this reaction can take place in other tissues, and reversal of this sequence, resulting in formation of UDP-galactose from glucose, occurs, particularly in the central nervous system, during synthesis of some galactolipids. Excessive intake of galactose can lead to toxicity. The capacity of the enzyme systems

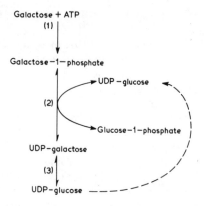

Fig. 3.4 Galactose metabolism. Enzymes: (1) galactokinase, (2) hexose-1-phosphate uridyl transferase, (3) UDP-glucose epimerase.

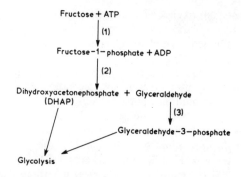

Fig. 3.5 Fructose metabolism. Enzymes: (1) fructokinase, (2) aldolase, (3) may be several steps; exact pathway still controversial.

to metabolize galactose can be exceeded, leading to the build-up of galactose and intermediates of the pathway. Increased levels of UDP-galactose may interfere with other normal metabolic pathways requiring uridine compounds. The high level of circulating galactose is thought to be responsible for the cataracts observed in the eyes of subjects fed high amounts of galactose. The cataracts are probably a result of osmotic changes occurring when galactose, readily permeable to membranes, enters the lens and is converted to a non-permeating compound, dulcitol, which has a strong osmotic effect [26].

Galactosaemia is a hereditary metabolic disorder in which there is an absence of hexose-1-phosphate uridyltransferase, leading to the accumulation of gal-1-phosphate when galactose is present in the diet. Until withdrawal from a diet of galactose-containing foods, an infant with galactosaemia will display symptoms of vomiting, diarrhea, and jaundice. Cataracts and mental deficiency may also develop. There is an alternate pathway for formation of UDP-gal, namely, UTP + gal-1-P ↔ UDP-gal + PPᵢ, but this enzyme is developmental and only weakly active in neo-

natal tissue. At full development the enzyme does not exceed one-sixth the activity of hexose-1-phosphate uridyltransferase but is sufficient to allow the adult galactosaemic an improved tolerance of galactose [27].

The normal metabolism of fructose occurs primarily in liver and follows the pathway shown in Fig. 3.5. Aldolase in muscle will split F-1-P but only 1/50 as rapidly as it will split FDP. Though some fructose can be converted to F6P by hexokinase in peripheral tissues, the K_m of hexokinase for fructose is high while that for glucose is low. Thus, the direct utilization of fructose by peripheral tissues is minimal.

In the metabolic disease of fructose intolerance, the activity of liver aldolase is below normal even with FDP as substrate, and only about 4% of normal for F1P. The resulting accumulation of F1P has been shown to inhibit the activity of other glycolytic enzymes, leading to hypoglycaemia and its accompanying symptoms [28]. Removal of fructose and sucrose from the diet eliminates the symptoms.

In the normal liver, fructose joins the glycolytic pathway as triose phosphates, below phosphofructokinase, the enzyme generally regarded as rate-limiting in glycolysis. Consequently, there is an unusual increase in levels of glycolytic intermediates [29]. These intermediates can move up the gluconeogenic pathway to glycogen or glucose or down the path of glycolysis, producing large amounts of lactate. Associated with high fructose intakes are increases in the activities of the enzymes concerned with lipogenesis, namely fatty acid synthetase, citrate lyase, malic enzyme, and G6P dehydrogenase (HMP pathway) [30]. Given these increases and the fact that lactate is lipogenic as well as glucogenic, there is a great increase in fatty acid synthesis and lipogenesis [30]. Also thriving under these conditions is cholesterol synthesis. These consequences are more notable in species such as man that synthesize lipids primarily in the liver. It is these increases in fat and cholesterol synthesis that have implicated sucrose and fructose in heart disease [31].

Also accompanying fructose feeding is a depletion of liver ATP, probably as a result of phosphorylation of fructose [32]. The high level of F1P may indicate that aldolase, which in liver is equally effective at attacking FDP and F1P, is rate-limiting in fructose metabolism and may be inhibited by some of the metabolites produced during fructose metabolism.

In some manner the liver is able to distinguish between the various forms of incoming carbohydrate and to alter enzyme activity selectively to favor glucose formation. When glucose is the primary dietary carbohydrate, very little is metabolized by the liver, and the two terminal enzymes of gluconeogenesis, FDPase and G6Pase, are vitually unaltered. When dietary galactose is high, however, liver G6Pase activity is increased, but FDPase is unchanged. To be converted to blood glucose, galactose must become G6P but not FDP. For fructose to be converted to blood glucose, it must pass through both FDPase and G6Pase. Therefore, as might be expected, when dietary fructose is high, liver FDPase and G6Pase both increase in activity [33].

None of these three carbohydrates has any effect on PEPCK, a gluconeogenic enzyme observed to increase in starvation or with carbohydrate-free diets. For conversion to blood glucose, fructose, galactose, and glucose do not undergo the reaction catalyzed by PEPCK, whereas the glucogenic substances entering the liver during starvation or carbohydrate-free diets must pass through PEPCK. It is not presently understood by what mechanisms the liver is able selectively to alter its enzyme activity according to the source of its glucose precursors.

References

[1] Szepesi, B. and Freedland, R. A. (1967), *J. Nutr.*, **93**, 301; and (1968), *J. Nutr.*, **94**, 463.

[2] Brambila, S. and Hill, F. W. (1966), *J. Nutr.*, **88**, 84.

[3] Painter, N. S. and Burkitt, D. P. (1971), *Br. Med. J.*, **2**, 450.

[4] Owen, O. E., Morgan, A. P., Kemp, H. G., Sullivan, J. M., Herrera, M. P. and Cahill, G. F. Jr. (1967), *J. Clin. Invest.*, **46**, 1589.

[5] Stoll, R. W., Touber, J. L., Menahan, L. A. and Williams, R. H. (1970), *Proc. Soc. for Experimental Biology and Medicine*, **133**, 894.

[6] Newsholme, E. A., Rolleston, F. S. and Taylor, K. (1968), *Biochem. J.*, **106**, 193; and England, P. J. and Randle, P. J. (1967), *Biochem. J.*, **105**, 907.

[7] Hornbrook, K. R., Burch, H. B. and Lowry, O. H. (1965), *Biochem. Biophys. Res. Commun.*, **18**, 206.

[8] Villar-Palasi, C. and Larner, J. (1961), *Arch. Biochem. Biophys.*, **94**, 436.

[9] Krebs, E. G. (1972), In *Current Topics in Cellular Regulation*, V. **5**, 99, Academic Press, New York.

[10] Randle, P. J., Denton, R. M. and England, P. J. (1968), In *Metabolic Roles of Citrate*, 87, Academic Press, New York.

[11] Clark, M. G., Kneer, N. M., Bosch, A. L. and Lardy, H. A. (1974), *J. Biol. Chem.*, 249, 5695.

[12] Garland, P. B. and Randle, P. J. (1964), *Biochem. J.*, 91, 6C.

[13] Portenhauser, R. and Wieland, O. (1974), *Eur. J. Biochem.*, 31, 308.

[14] Siess, E. A. and Wieland, O. (1972), *Eur. J. Biochem.*, 26, 96.

[15] Wieland, O., Siess, E., Schulze-Wothmar, F. H., Funcke, H. J. V. and Winton, B. (1971), *Arch. Biochem. Biophys.*, 143, 593.

[16] Wieland, O. H. and Portenhauser, R. (1974), *Eur. J. Biochem.*, 45, 577.

[17] Scrutton, M. C. and Utter, M. F. (1967), *J. biol. Chem.*, 242, 1723.

[18] Lardy, H. A., Foster, D. O., Skiago, E. and Ray, P. D. (1964), In *Advances in Enzyme Regulation*, (ed) Weber, G., II, 2.

[19] Shrago, E., Young, J. W. and Lardy, H. A. (1967), *Science*, 158, 1572.

[20] Hanson, R. W. and Garber, H. J. (1972), *Am. J. Clin. Nutr.*, 25, 1010.

[21] Johnson, D. C., Brunsvold, R. A., Ekit, K. H. and Ray, P. D. (1973), *J. biol. Chem.*, 248, 763.

[22] Longshaw, I. D., Bowen, N. L. and Pogson, C. I. (1972), *Eur. J. Biochem.*, 25, 366.

[23] Peng, Y-S., Brooks, M., Elson, C. and Shrago, E. (1973), *J. Nutr.*, 103, 1489.

[24] Ross, B. D., Hems, R., Freedland, R. A. and Krebs, H. A. (1967), *Biochem. J.*, 105, 869.

[25] Black, A. L., Luick, J., Moller, F. and Anand, R. (1966), *J. biol. Chem.*, 241, 5233.

[26] Gitzelmann, R. (1967), *Ped. Res.*, 1, 14.

[27] Isselbacher, K. J. (1957), *Science*, 126, 652.

[28] Cornblath, M., Rosenthal, I. M., Reisner, S. H., Wybregt, S. H. and Crane, R. K. (1963), *New Eng. J. Med.*, 269, 1271.

[29] Burch, H. B., Lowry, O. H., Meinhardt, L., Max, P., Jr. and Chyl, K. J. (1970), *J. biol. Chem.*, 245, 2092.

[30] Zakim, D. (1973), *Prog. Biochem. Pharmacol.*, 8, 161.

[31] Yudkin, J. (1967), *Am. J. Clin. Nutr.*, 20, 108.

[32] Bode, C., Schmacher, H., Goebell, H. Zelder, O. and Pelzel, H. (1971), *Hormone Metab. Res.*, 3, 289.

[33] Freedland, R. A. and Harper, A. E. (1959), *J. biol. Chem.*, 234, 1350.

Recommended reading

Newsholme, E. A. and Start, C. (1973), *Regulation in Metabolism*. John Wiley & Sons, Ltd., London.

Zakim, D. (1973), *Prog. biochem. Pharmacol.*, 8, 161–188.

Stanbury, J. B., Wyngaarden, J. B. and Fredrickson, D. S. (1972), In The Metabolic Basis of Inherited Disease, pp. 83–219, McGraw-Hill, New York.

Fain, J. (1974), Mode of action of insulin, In *Biochemistry*, Series One, vol. 8, pp. 1–23, (ed.) Rickenberg, H. V., Butterworths, London.

4 Lipids and fatty acids

4.1 Physical properties

Lipids can be defined as organic substances originating in living matter, which are insoluble in water but are soluble in non-polar solvents such as alcohol, ether, chloroform, and benzene. Such a definition includes free fatty acids, alcohols (other than glycerol, which is water soluble), sterols (e.g. cholesterol), some hydrocarbons such as the carotenoids, and the fat soluble vitamins D, E, and K. Of major quantitative significance in plant and animal tissues are: 1) the neutral fats or triglycerides, which consist of three fatty acids esterified with glycerol, 2) the phospholipids, containing two fatty acids and inorganic phosphate esterified with glycerol, often with a nitrogenous base such as choline or ethanolamine also esterified to the phosphate, and 3) the cholesterol esters.

The physical and chemical characteristics of many of these lipids are determined largely by the number of carbon atoms in the fatty acid moieties and by the number of carbon—carbon double bonds. The fatty acids of most plant and animal lipids contain an even number of carbon atoms. Most animal fats are saturated (i.e. have no double bonds), while most plant lipids contain unsaturated and poly-unsaturated (more than two double bonds) fatty acids.

Lipids can be formed in the body from carbohydrate, protein, or lipid precursors. However, certain essential poly-unsaturated fatty acids cannot be formed *de novo* by the animal body and consequently must be included in the diet. Linoleic acid, with 18 carbons and three double bonds, and arachidonic acid, with 20 carbons and four double bonds, are regarded as the essential fatty acids, since either is able to overcome the symptoms of essential fatty acid deficiency. However, the body can make arachidonic acid if provided with linoleic acid. Essential fatty acids are important for maintaining cell membrane structure and in particular, capillary wall integrity. They also are thought to be required for the efficient transport and metabolism of cholesterol.

Unsaturated and, particularly, poly-unsaturated fatty acids are susceptible to chemical oxidation by free radicals, which can be formed during metabolism or from exogenous agents, such as ozone. The oxidation of these fatty acids when they are constituents of the membrane can lead to loss of some of the biological properties of the membrane. Some investigators have associated changes of this nature with aging. On the shelf and *in vitro,* free radical oxidation of lipids can be lessened by addition of an antioxidant, a compound which can accept a free radical and thereby terminate the chain reaction. Attempts have been made to apply antioxidants *in vivo* to minimize membrane damage by free radical oxidation and thereby to slow the aging process. Vitamin E, a fat soluble vitamin with *in vitro* antioxidant properties, is popularly employed for this purpose. To date, however, there is no incontrovertible evidence that the aging process is deterred by such treatment.

4.2 General functions

Lipids, in the form of cholesterol, cholesterol esters, and phospholipids, comprise a large component of membranes, including not only the cellular membrane, but those of cell organelles such as mitochondria, lysosomes, and endoplasmic reticula. The phospholipids usually contain one or more unsaturated fatty acids, which, through lowering the melting point of the lipids, keep the membranes fluid and flexible rather than fixed and rigid. (Tallow, which is formed of triglycerides of saturated fatty acids, is more solid.) Cellular membranes are pictured as a fluid sea of lipid with proteins floating within as icebergs. The proteins may float on either side of the lipid portion of the membrane or penetrate the lipid portion entirely (see Fig. 4.1).

In addition to contributing to cell membrane structure, lipids provide metabolites for the formation of the hormone-like prostaglandins, which may be important metabolic regulators. The prostaglandins can be formed in many tissues and appear to exert their hormone-like effects also on a large variety of tissues. Some have catabolic effects and others have anabolic effects. In several tissues, prostaglandins may modify the activity of other hormones. The relationship of the essential fatty acids and their derivatives to several prostaglandins can be seen in Fig. 4.2. The study of the roles of prostaglandins in physiology and metabolism is one of the newest and most prolific areas of current interest and research.

Other functions of lipids include providing protective insulation and serving as the body's largest reservoir of energy storage. Two features of lipid make it an ideal storage form of energy for living things on the move: it has a high energy density and is hydrophobic. Carbohy-

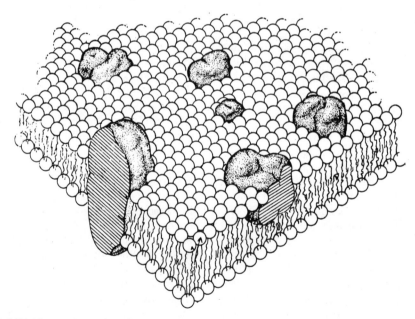

Fig. 4.1 Fluid mosaic model of membrane structure, (Adapted from S. J. Singer and G. L. Nicolson, (1972), Science, 175, 720—731.)

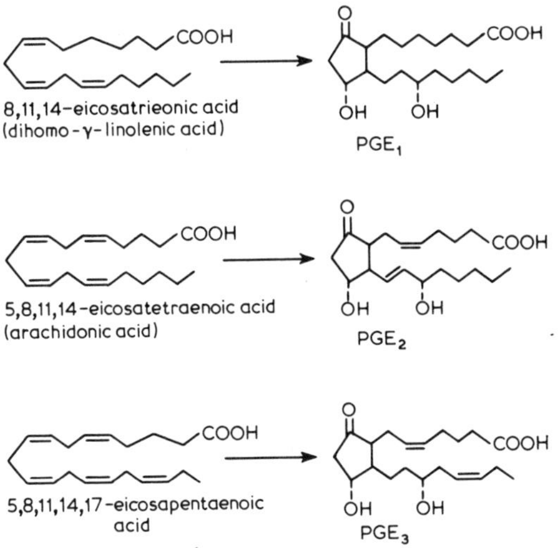

8,11,14-eicosatrieonic acid
(dihomo-γ-linolenic acid) → PGE$_1$

5,8,11,14-eicosatetraenoic acid
(arachidonic acid) → PGE$_2$

5,8,11,14,17-eicosapentaenoic
acid → PGE$_3$

Fig. 4.2 Relationship of fatty acids and prostaglandins. PGE — prostaglandin E. Other naturally occurring prostaglandins are grouped as prostaglandin A, B and F. Groups E and F appear to be the most important biologically.

drate, while having half the calories per gram, is hydrophilic and is stored with almost an equal weight of water. Therefore, when carbohydrate (e.g. glycogen) is the storage form, a given amount of energy requires 4 times the weight needed to store that same energy as lipid. For the sedentary clam or oyster, mobility is relatively unimportant and glycogen provides a suitable form for excess energy storage. But for the foraging animal or the wind-borne plant seed, the need to move demands a lighter energy storage form.

A commonly attributed advantage to lipid as a storage form is its greater yield of metabolic water (i.e. water produced during complete combustion of metabolic substances) as compared to carbohydrate. It is true that a gram of fat yields more metabolic water than a gram of carbohydrate. However, the body burns its energy stores not on a gram basis, but according to the number of ATPs yielded. Comparing storage forms of lipid and carbohydrate, we find that tripalmitin yields 0.12 water molecules per ATP while glycogen produces 0.132. Thus, the idea that lipid is preferable as an energy storage form because of its high potential for yielding metabolic water is invalid.

4.3 Digestion and disposition of dietary lipids

When dietary fats are consumed, the triglycerides become partially emulsified in the gut through combination with conjugated bile salts and are then subject to the hydrolytic action of pancreatic lipase. The resulting fatty acids and monoglycerides are absorbed by the intestinal mucosa. There the monoglycerides containing short-chain fatty acids are further hydrolized and the glycerol and short-chain fatty acids are absorbed by the mesenteric blood. The long-chain fatty acids are re-esterified into triglycerides within the mucosa and from there pass into the lymphatics as small particles complexed with protein, called chylomicrons. Thus, triglycerides formed of long-chain fatty acids by-pass the liver when they enter the circulation. The advantage of this by-pass is a sparing of fatty acids for use by the extra-hepatic tissues.

After the triglycerides have entered the blood via the thoracic duct, their hydrolysis is catalyzed by lipoprotein lipase, an enzyme thought to be associated with capillary walls. The fatty acids can then be absorbed by adjacent tissues for use as energy, membrane formation, or storage. The activity of lipoprotein lipase varies in different organs and tissues according to the nutritional and hormonal state of the animal. During starvation, for instance, when lipid storage is of small importance, lipoprotein lipase activity in adipose tissue decreases greatly [1, 2]. On the other hand, the activity increases in heart and muscle, which burn fatty acids for energy in the absence of carbohydrate energy sources [3]. Re-feeding a high carbohydrate diet causes the opposite changes: a drop in lipoprotein lipase activity in

31

heart, which can now burn carbohydrate, and an increase in the activity in adipose tissue, which can now store dietary lipid and lipid synthesized in the liver from dietary carbohydrate [1, 2].

The presence or absence of carbohydrate affects not only the activity of lipoprotein lipase and hence the availability of fatty acids for triglyceride synthesis in adipose tissue, but it also affects the ability of adipose tissue to form the α-glycerolphosphate (αGP) needed for triglyceride formation. Glycerol is formed in adipose tissue upon hydrolysis of triglycerides, a process which occurs continually though not at a constant rate. But the adipose cell has practically no ability to phosphorylate glycerol and must synthesize the needed αGP from dihydroxyacetonephosphate (DHAP), an intermediate of glycolysis [4]. Thus, lipid metabolism and carbohydrate metabolism cannot be entirely divorced from one another.

4.4 Lipid synthesis

The enzymes concerned in *de novo* lipid synthesis, including acetyl CoA carboxylase, fatty acid synthetase, citrate lyase, and enzymes generating NADPH, such as glucose-6-phosphate dehydrogenase (the first enzyme of the HMP pathway) and malic enzyme, are greatly influenced by the quantities of fat and carbohydrate in the diet. During consumpton of a high carbohydrate diet, these enzymes show large increases in activity, allowing for the storage of excess dietary energy as body fat [5]. Conversely, during starvation or feeding of very high fat diets — conditions not requiring *de novo* fatty acid synthesis — these enzyme activities are low [5]. (With a high fat diet, storage of excess energy can be accomplished by directly storing dietary fat.)

The form of dietary carbohydrate also influences the lipogenic enzymes. When sucrose replaces dietary glucose or starch, there is a marked increase in the enzymes associated with lipogenesis, particularly in liver [6]. In addition, the fructose moiety, entering glycolysis beyond the regulation point at phosphofructokinase, can provide increased substrate for the liver to carry on lipogenesis. This increased potential for lipogenic activity in liver may be more detrimental than a comparable increase in adipose tissue, since the liver is the primary site of cholesterol synthesis. It has been observed that after a high fructose diet, the level of circulating lipids in the form of lipoproteins and liver cholesterol is markedly greater than after a diet high in starch or glucose [7, 8].

The major site of *de novo* synthesis of fatty acids is species dependent [9, 10]. In the rat, about two-thirds of the fatty acid synthesis takes place in adipose tissue and the remaining one-third in liver. In the pig, nearly all occurs in adipose tissue. In the chicken, on the other hand, it appears that nearly all fatty acids are synthesized in the liver and transported to adipose tissue for storage. In man, the situation is still not certain, but most of the evidence indicates that, as in the chicken, most fatty acids are synthesized in the liver and transported to adipose tissue for storage [10, 11]. Consequently, the chicken may be a better model than the rat or pig for studies of lipid metabolism that are to be related to man.

Regardless of the particular site, the immediate substrate for fatty acid synthesis is acetyl Coenzyme A. Acetyl CoA is readily produced from pyruvate, which can arise from lactate, glucose, amino acids, etc. However, pyruvate dehydrogenase is a mitochondrial enzyme and forms acetyl CoA within the mitochondria, whereas fatty acid synthesis is a cytoplasmic process. Acetyl CoA is too large a molecule to traverse the mitochondrial membrane. Consequently, acetyl CoA must change compartments by a more indirect mechanism.

One possible means is the hydrolysis of acetyl CoA within the mitochondria and the subsequent leakage of acetate into the cytoplasm where it could be reactivated to form cytoplasmic acetyl CoA. Activation of each acetate costs two high energy phosphates and such a system would make fatty acid synthesis very expensive. Furthermore, the activities of the enzymes that hydrolyze acetyl CoA in the mitochondria are too low to account for fatty acid synthesis rates [12]. Hydrolysis of acetyl CoA therefore cannot be a major mechanism of transfer.

A second possible means of transfer of acetyl CoA to the cytoplasm is one similar to that used to transport long-chain fatty acids into the mitochondria: namely, a carnitine derivative of acetate which can traverse the membrane and transfer the acetate to coenzyme A in the cytoplasm. Here again the enzyme systems appear to be insufficient to account for maximal rates of fatty acid synthesis.

The most likely mechanism of transfer of acetyl CoA from the mitochondria is the intra-mitochondrial formation of citrate, which can permeate the mitochondrial membrane. In the cytoplasm, citrate can be cleaved by citrate lyase to form acetyl CoA and oxaloacetate, with the cost of one high-energy phosphate per acetyl unit. In this case the enzymes are high enough to account for fatty acid synthesis rates [12].

Experiments to date indicate that the transport of acetate from mitochondria to cytoplasm occurs by prior conversion to citrate or isocitrate [13]. Because the citrate concentration in mitochondria is 15 times that of isocitrate, it appears that citrate is the major transport form. This mechanism is well co-ordinated with the many regulatory roles of citrate. When cell energy is high, the citric acid cycle is blocked at isocitrate dehydrogenase, causing an increase in concentrations of isocitrate and citrate, and passage of citrate to the cytoplasm. When this occurs in muscle cells, the increased cytoplasmic citrate magnifies the ATP inhibition of phosphofructokinase, thereby slowing

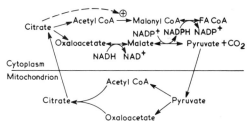

Fig. 4.3 Role of citrate in fatty acid metabolism. Citrate is a positive effector of acetyl CoA carboxylase and a precursor of both cytoplasmic acetyl CoA and oxaloacetate, which through malic dehydrogenase (NAD) and malic enzyme (NADP) can be used for an effective trans-hydrogenation from NADH to NADPH, a cofactor required for fatty acid synthesis.

glycolysis. In liver and adipose cells, which can use excess energy to make fat, higher cytoplasmic citrate allows citrate lyase to manifest its potential in forming acetyl CoA for fatty acid synthesis (Fig. 4.3). Citrate is also a potent activator of acetyl CoA carboxylase (AcCoA + CO_2 + ATP → malonyl CoA + ADP + P_i), which may be the rate-limiting enzyme of fatty acid synthesis [14]. When citrate is cleaved by citrate lyase, the resulting oxaloacetate is rapidly reduced with NADH to form malate. Malate can then be acted upon by malic enzyme to provide pyruvate, CO_2, and NADPH. Therefore, citrate transport not only transfers acetyl CoA to the cytoplasm but also provides a means to convert NADH to NADPH. Two NADPH molecules are required per acetyl moiety incorporated into fatty acids beyond the first acetyl unit, and the cleavage of citrate can ultimately provide one of these. The other is provided by other systems such as the hexose monophosphate pathway. Indeed, estimations using tritiated glucose and malate indicate that about one-half the NADPH needed for lipid synthesis comes from malic enzyme and about one-half from HMP [15]. Thus, citrate plays a central role in lipid metabolism.

One might ask at this point why a high fat diet does not cause increased fatty acid synthesis, since a high fat diet should produce a high energy state, high acetyl CoA levels from catabolism of dietary fat, and consequently high concentrations of citrate. The answer is that acetyl CoA carboxylase, the apparently limiting enzyme of fatty acid synthesis, is inhibited by fatty acyl CoA and by free fatty acids [16], which would both be abundant with a high fat diet. Although the lipogenic enzymes are decreased during feeding of a high fat diet, the inhibition of acetyl CoA carboxylase may be a primary cause of depressed fatty acid synthesis. A change in concentrations of fatty acids or fatty acyl CoA can be manifested rapidly, thereby providing acute control, whereas the change in enzyme activities requires more time and might serve as a long term regulator.

We noted earlier that certain enzymes involved in lipogenesis increase under dietary conditions which would provide excess substrate for fat synthesis. It has been controversial as to whether the observed increase in glucose-6-phosphate dehydrogenase (G6PD), malic enzyme, and citrate lyase are necessary for the accompanying increased rates of fatty acid synthesis or whether they are merely a reflection of the greater fat synthesis. Under most conditions, the activities of G6PD and malic enzyme are adequate to produce all the NADPH required for maximum rates of fatty acid synthesis. Furthermore, the ratio of NADPH to NADP is always very high, even when lipogenesis is occurring at its maximum rate [17]. It appears in fact that G6PD is inhibited by high NADPH and that the inhibition can be alleviated by utilization of NADPH in such processes as fatty acid synthesis. In tissue preparations, NADPH has been oxidized to NADP by addition of phenazine methosulfate, resulting in a 3-fold increase in the contribution of the HMP pathway [18]. Thus it appears that the limiting factor in NADPH generation is the utilization of NADPH already formed and not the enzymes required for its formation. Thus the responses of G6PD and malic enzyme to various diets are probably consequences rather than causes of fatty acid synthesis rates.

Citrate lyase activity also seems to be an indicator of lipogenesis but not a cause. This was shown experimentally in starved animals, which, if unfed, had very low rates of lipogenesis. Rates of fatty acid synthesis were monitored following feeding. The increases in fatty acid synthesis were observed to occur before changes in enzymes associated with lipogenesis would occur [19].

4.5 Storage and release of fatty acids

Considering the roles of glucose in *de novo* synthesis of fatty acids and in triglyceride storage in adipose tissue, and recalling the close interrelationship of glucose and insulin, we should not be surprised to learn that insulin is of major importance in lipid metabolism. Indeed, adipose tissue is one of the tissues most sensitive to insulin with regard to cell permeability in glucose. When a high carbohydrate diet is consumed, not only does the blood glucose level rise, but insulin output increases. This allows a greater portion of the glucose to enter adipose cells, where it can be converted to fatty acids and αGP and stored as fat. In contrast, with a high fat diet, when glucose and insulin are both low, storage of fat is more difficult. Although fatty acids are available to the cells through action of lipoprotein lipase, the adipose cells have a shortage of glucose and therefore of αGP, thereby limiting the formation of triglycerides.

Animals trained to eat their entire day's food in a single meal have been shown to become fatter than animals consuming the same amount of food in several meals throughout the day [20]. With a single meal, absorption continues at the maximal rate for a longer period and the resulting high blood glucose maintains

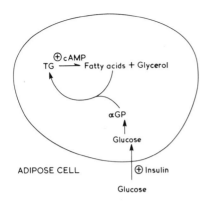

Fig. 4.4 Triglyceride–fatty acid cycle.

insulin output, allowing a greater proportion of the glucose to enter the adipose cells.

The formation and hydrolysis of triglycerides are intimately related processes in adipose tissue and create what might be called a triglyceride-fatty acid cycle. Within an adipose cell, fatty acids and glycerol can be formed by hydrolysis of triglyceride. If αGP is available (from metabolism of glucose) triglycerides can be reformed by esterification of the αGP and fatty acids. If αGP is not available, the concentration of fatty acids will build up and fatty acids will be released into the blood. The rates of formation and hydrolysis of triglycerides are regulated not only by glucose availability but by the level of cellular cyclic AMP (cAMP), which responds to many hormones, including insulin (Fig. 4.4).

During starvation, for instance, blood glucose drops to a low level at which it is maintained by a homeostatic mechanism. Insulin also falls to a very low level. The low insulin level and changes in other hormones cause an increase in cAMP in adipose cells. The higher cAMP concentration causes hormone-sensitive lipase to become activated, and the rate of hydrolysis of triglycerides increases. Because glucose availability is low, re-esterification of

the fatty acids resulting from hydrolysis is limited. Therefore the fatty acids are released into the blood where they become bound to albumin. The albumin-bound non-esterified fatty acids (NEFAs) can travel to other tissues where they can be used for fuel. In the liver they can also form ketone bodies, which account for nearly 80% of the fatty acids catabolized in the liver under starvation conditions [21]. Muscle, the other primary user of NEFAs, will burn fatty acids and ketone bodies in preference to glucose, thereby sparing the limited glucose supply. Fatty acids protect glucose by decreasing its permeability into cells. Also, by creating higher concentrations of citrate and ATP, the fatty acids inhibit glycolysis at PFK. Further, they cause a conversion of pyruvate dehydrogenase from the active to the inactive form.

4.6 Ketone body metabolism

Ketone bodies, unlike fatty acids, provide an alternate fuel source for brain, replacing up to three-fourths of the brain's glucose requirement [22]. Since they readily cross the mitochondrial membrane, ketone bodies are more rapidly activated in muscle than are fatty acids. Liver has no activating enzymes for ketone bodies and therefore does not compete with other tissues for their use.

Along with these advantages, ketone bodies can have some detrimental effects. When blood ketone levels are markedly elevated, the kidney is not able to reabsorb all the ketone bodies. The excreted ketone bodies represent a loss of energy from the body. Furthermore, since the kidney can acidify the urine only to pH 4.5–5, the approximate pK of the ketone bodies, only half the excreted ketone bodies can be in the acid form. The other half must be accompanied by a cation, normally sodium. This leads to a depletion of sodium, followed by a depletion of potassium, calcium and other minerals. The energy loss plus the acid-base balance problem

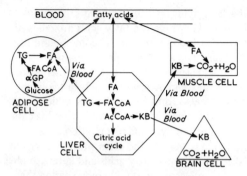

Fig. 4.5 Overall view of lipid metabolism. FA − fatty acid, FACoA − fatty acyl co-enzyme A, TG − triglyceride, KB − ketone body.

which occur in ketonuria can be a major cause of death in untreated diabetics.

All of the processes involved in the disposition of NEFAs − oxidation to carbon dioxide and water, conversion to ketone bodies, or storage as fat − are continually taking place, but their balance depends on the hormonal state and dietary intake of the animal. Shifts in the balance of these processes are generally to the animal's benefit, allowing adaptation to the situation (Fig. 4.5). One shift that appears to be to the detriment of the animal, however, occurs with the consumption of alcohol. In alcoholics and even in 'social drinkers' there is increased lipid deposition in the liver. Whether this fatty liver syndrome is the cause of cirrhosis of the liver is controversial, but the one is often followed by the other.

4.7 Effects of alcohol

Fatty liver in alcoholics was formerly thought to be a consequence of inadquate dietary protein intake and the resultant shortage of proteins for transporting lipid from the liver to the periphery. But the metabolism of alcohol itself affects lipid synthesis. The liver is the main site of alcohol metabolism and, in man, is also the major organ for both fatty acid synthesis and metabolism of NEFAs from adipose tissue. When alcohol is metabolized, NADH is produced in the cytoplasm and there is a notable increase in the ratio of NADH to NAD. This increase affects the equilibria of many reactions involving this coenzyme. One such reaction affected is:−

$$DHAP + NADH \leftrightarrow \alpha GP + NAD.$$

When DHAP is formed in the normal process of gluconeogenesis, the higher concentration of NADH shifts the equilibrium to formation of αGP. In the presence of alcohol, the αGP concentration of liver has been observed to increase 5-fold or more [23]. The significance of this change occurs in the removal of one of the major controls of fatty acid synthesis. Ordinarily the long-chain fatty acyl CoA, the product of fatty acid synthesis and of triglyceride breakdown, inhibits acetyl CoA carboxylase, thus preventing the synthesis of fatty acids during times of lipid catabolism and regulating the rate of synthesis during times of anabolism. When αGP is abundantly present to act as an acceptor of fatty acyl CoA, however, fatty acyl CoA cannot accumulate and its regulatory effect is removed, thus causing the development of fatty liver [24].

References

[1] Hollenberg, C. H. (1959), *Am. J. Physiol.,* **197**, 667.

[2] Robinson, D. S. (1960), *J. Lipid Res.,* **1**, 332.

[3] Borensztajn, J., Otway, S. and Robinson, D. S. (1970), *J. Lipid Res.,* **11**, 102.

[4] Robinson, J. and Newsholme, E. A. (1967), *Biochem. J.,* **104**, 2C.

[5] Tepperman, H. M. and Tepperman, J. (1964), *Am. J. Physiol.,* **206**, 357.

[6] Fitch, W. M. and Chaikoff, I. L. (1960), *J. biol. Chem.,* **235**, 554.

[7] Burchdorfer, K. R., Kari-Kari, B. P. B., Khan, I. H. and Yudkin, J. (1972), *Nutr. Metab.*, **14**, 228.

[8] Vrana, A., Fabry, P. and Kazdova, L. (1973), *Nutr. Metab.*, **15**, 305.

[9] Shafir, E. and Wertheimer, E. (1965), In *Handbook of Physiology*, Section 5: Adipose Tissue, (eds) Reynold, A. E. and Cahill, G. F., Jr., **417**; O'Hea, E. K. and Leveille, G. A. (1969), *J. Nutr.*, **99**, 338; and Muiruri, K. L. and Leveille, G. A. (1970), *International J. Biochem.*, **1**, 254.

[10] Shrago, E., Glennon, J. A. and Gordon, E. S. (1971), *Metabolism,* **20**, 54.

[11] Patel, M. S., Owen, O. E., Goldman, L. I. and Hanson, R. W. (1975), *Metabolism,* **24**, 161.

[12] Spencer, A. F. and Lowenstein, J. M. (1962), *J. biol. Chem.*, **237**, 3640.

[13] Bartley, J., Abraham, S. and Chaikoff, I. L. (1965), *Biochem. Biophys. Res. Comm.*, **19**, 770.

[14] Martin, D. B. and Vagelos, P. R. (1962), *J. biol. Chem.*, **237**, 1787.

[15] Rognstad, R. and Katz, J. (1966), *Proc. natn. Acad. Sci.*, (USA), **55**, 1148.

[16] Numa, S., Ringelmann, E. and Lynn, F. (1965), *Biochem. Z.*, **343**, 243.

[17] Veech, R. L., Eggleston, L. V. and Krebs, H. A. (1969), *Biochem. J.*, **115**, 609.

[18] Katz, J. and Wals, P. A. (1971), *Arch. biochem. Biophys.*, **147**, 405.

[19] Sullivan, A. C., Miller, N. O., Wittman, J. S. III and Hamilton, J. G. (1971), *J. Nutr.*, **101**, 265.

[20] Leveille, G. A. (1970), *Illinois Res.*, **12**, 6.

[21] Krebs, H. A., Wallace, P. G., Hems, R. and Freedland, R. A. (1969), *Biochem. J.*, **112**, 595.

[22] Owen, O. E., Morgon, A. P., Kemp, H. G., Sullivan, J. M. Herrera, M. G. and Cahill, G. F., Jr. (1967), *J. Clin. Invest.*, **46**, 1589.

[23] Krebs, H. A., Freedland, R. A., Hems, R. and Stubbs, M. (1969), *Biochem. J.*, **112**, 117.

[24] Lieber, C. S. (1967), *Annual Rev. Med.*, **18**, 35.

Recommended reading

Newsholme, E. A. and Start, C. (1973), *Regulation in Metabolism.* John Wiley & Sons, Ltd., London.

Lowenstein, J. M. (1972), Is insulin involved in the rate of fatty acid synthesis? In *Handbook of Physiol.*, Section 7, *Endocrinology*, **1**, 415—424, Amer. Physiol. Soc., Washington, D.C.

Lapidus, M., Grant, N. H. and Alburn, H. E. (1968), *J. Lipid Res.*, **9**, 371—373.

Nakano, J. (1973), General pharmacology of prostaglandins, pp. 23—124 In *The Prostaglandins,* (ed) Cuthbert, M. F., William Heinemann Medical Books, Ltd., London.

5 Protein and amino acids

Protein occurs in all living things. Formed of amino acids bonded together in peptide linkage, proteins have a far greater potential for variability than do either carbohydrates or lipids. The combinations and permutations of the approximately twenty amino acids occurring in protein are legion, and the unique sequence and length of each protein gives it its conformation and makes it suitable for its particular function. Because of the many different proteins, the functions of protein are numerous: structural components, catalysts of chemical reactions (i.e. enzymes), transporting agents, hormonal messengers (e.g. insulin), osomotic regulators (e.g. albumin), buffers, etc.

5.1 Digestion and absorption

There is no dietary requirement of protein *per se*. The requirement is for the building materials to make protein. For certain bacteria, NH_3 and a carbon source suffice to allow the organism to construct amino acids and thence proteins. Most animals however, require at least part, if not all, of their nitrogen intake to be in the form of amino acids. These amino acids can occur in their free forms or can be bonded together in proteins. In naturally occurring food substances amino acids rarely are free but rather linked as protein.

Dietary proteins, because they are large molecules, do not cross the intestinal wall to any significant extent in the adult animal and cannot be used by the body even when introduced parenterally. Thus, to enter the circulation and to be utilized for protein synthesis, dietary protein must be hydrolyzed to its amino acids.

Denaturation of the protein molecule and some digestion by the enzyme pepsin occurs in the stomach, but the major site of protein digestion is the small intestine. There the protein is attacked by the proteolytic enzymes trypsin and chymotrypsin, and the peptide fragments by various peptidases. Trypsin and chymotrypsin enter the intestine from the pancreas as inactive forms, called zymogens, and are themselves activated in the small intestine by proteolytic cleavage. The pancreas is protected from proteolytic destruction by the inactivity of the zymogen, while the intestine is protected from the active proteinases by the mucous coating secreted by the intestinal wall.

The amino acids resulting from protein breakdown are absorbed by the intestine and enter the portal circulation. However, the concentrations of amino acids in the portal blood do not correspond entirely to the amino acid composition of the dietary protein. Part of this lack of correlation may be due to varying rates of absorption, but it is partly a result of transformation of certain amino acids to other forms during absorption. In particular, much of the aspartate and glutamate is converted to alanine [1]. Accordingly, aspartate and glutamate are usually in very low concentration in blood. In parenteral feeding studies, high levels of aspartate and glutamate have been found to be detrimental [2]. One possible explanation for these deleterious effects is the strong chelating action of the two dicarboxylic acids, which may limit the availability of essential divalent cations such as Ca^{++} and Mg^{++}. The so-called Chinese restaurant syndrome, headache and ill feeling after consumption of Chinese food, has been attributed to the relatively large quantities of monosodium glutamate used in Chinese cooking. Blood glutamate levels have been observed to rise after a meal in which monosodium glutamate has been used. It may be that the intestine's ability to convert glutamate to alanine is exceeded by the quantity of glutamate present in the food and a significant quantity of glutamate is absorbed without conversion.

5.2 Concept of essential amino acids

For protein synthesis to take place, all the amino acid building blocks must be present. The body is able to make some of the amino acids by transferring amino groups to certain intermediates of carbohydrate metabolism. Such amino acids, which can be formed in the body and need not be obtained directly from the diet have unfortunately been labelled 'nonessential'. Though they are not individually essential as dietary components, they are essential for protein synthesis.

The concept of an 'essential' amino acid was defined originally by Rose as an amino acid that must be included in the diet to obtain optimal growth [3]. Though optimal growth has most often been construed to mean maximal growth, it is not obvious that maximal growth is optimal. Now that more is known of the metabolism of amino acids, this problem of definition can be avoided by defining an essential amino acid as one whose carbon skeleton cannot by synthesized in the body and must therefore be provided by the diet.

The essential amino acids can be subdivided into two groups: those amino acids which must be provided by the diet in the L-form, the form that is used in protein synthesis, and those amino acids which can be provided as the L-form, the D-form, the α-keto derivative, or the α-hydroxy derivative. In most higher animals the first category includes only the two amino acids, L-lysine and L-threonine, whereas the second category contains leucine, isoleucine, valine, tryptophan, phenylalanine, and methionine. The two amino acids, tyrosine and cysteine, are not regarded as essential because they can be made in the body from phenylalanine and methionine, respectively. However, this is the only source for their synthesis. In early stages of development, higher animals appear to require also arginine and histidine. Though the enzymatic machinery to synthesize these amino acids does exist, the rate of their production apparently cannot meet the demand made by protein synthesis for maximal growth.

Determining the amount of an amino acid needed by an animal requires, in addition to a criterion of adequacy, the awareness of interrelationships between certain of the amino acids and other nutrients. When tyrosine is present in the diet, the requirement of phenylalanine is lower than when tyrosine is absent. If tyrosine is supplied, phenylalanine need not be used to form tyrosine. Thus, tyrosine is said to 'spare' phenylalanine. Likewise, cysteine spares methionine. The vitamin niacin also spares tryptophan, since tryptophan can be converted to NAD.

The amounts of the essential amino acids required for growth or for maintenance vary greatly one from another. The disparities reflect the frequencies of their appearance in body proteins and the differing rates of their catabolism.

5.3 Protein quality

The quality of a dietary protein can be estimated by how nearly its amino acid profile matches the amino acid requirements. However, an additional factor must be considered in determining protein quality, and that is the availability of the amino acids for absorption. During food preparation, certain amino acids contained in a protein may be destroyed or rendered unavailable. One which is particularly subject to alteration during heat treatment is lysine. With high heat, the aldehyde groups of carbohydrate present in the food will bind to the ϵ-amino group of the lysine residues in the protein molecule, making the lysine nutritionally unavailable. This is known as the Browning reaction. In grain proteins, lysine is the amino acid in shortest supply relative to man's requirement. Therefore, losing its availability through processing is a matter for concern.

No naturally occurring protein entirely matches an animal's amino acid requirement. There is in a protein then one amino acid that is lowest with respect to its requirement. That one is referred to as the 'limiting' amino acid of the protein. Relative to man's requirement, lysine is the limiting amino acid in grain proteins, whereas methionine is the limiting amino acid in legumes and milk.

If the protein in a diet contains all the essential amino acids and enough of the protein is fed to provide a young animal with adequate amounts of the most limiting amino acid, the animal can grow. When the dietary protein is reduced, there comes a point when the amount of the most limiting amino acid is insufficient to maintain a high rate of protein synthesis, and growth becomes retarded. Supplementing the diet with the limiting amino acid will overcome the retardation. However, if two or more amino acids are nearly equally limiting, addition of only one may cause no improvement and may even be detrimental.

Some proteins, such as egg protein, contain such high quantities of essential amino acids that, as the amount of protein in the diet is reduced, total nitrogen for making non-essential amino acids becomes limiting. The growth

retardation due to insufficient nitrogen can be overcome by supplementation with non-essential amino acids.

5.4 Non-protein functions of amino acids

It has been stated that the primary need for dietary protein is for amino acids to build body proteins, which are continually turning over, even in the non-growing adult animal. However, amino acids have other functions as well. They are precursors for many hormones, such as thyroxine, epinephrine, serotonin, and γ-aminobutyric acid. They also contribute to

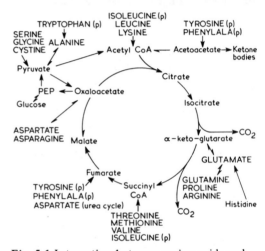

Fig. 5.1 Interaction between amino acids and citric acid cycle. Amino acids that *directly* produce acetyl CoA or acetoacetate are ketogenic. In the case of leucine and lysine, the amino acids are wholly ketogenic, whereas those amino acids marked (p) are only partially ketogenic. Amino acids which enter the metabolic scheme as pyruvate or citric acid cycle intermediates are glucogenic (i.e. can produce a *net* synthesis of glucose). Those amino acids marked (p) are partially glucogenic. All glucogenic amino acids, regardless of whether they are completely or partially glucogenic, can theoretically yield 1 mole of glucose per 2 moles of amino acid.

the synthesis of other important nitrogenous compounds such as purines, pyrimidines, hemes, and nitrogenous bases for phospholipids. In excess, the amino acids from dietary protein can be converted to carbohydrate or to lipid for storage of energy, or they can be burned for energy directly without storage.

Amino acids, whether from dietary sources or from catabolism of body proteins, are an important source of glucose. Of the twenty amino acids occurring in protein, eighteen are wholly or partially glucogenic (Fig. 5.1). When the diet lacks carbohydrate but provides protein, the glucose necessary to maintain glucose-dependent systems can be formed from the amino acids in the dietary protein. During times of starvation, amino acids from body protein are converted to glucose. Although there is no 'storage protein', no reservoir for the storage of excess dietary protein as there is for lipid and carbohydrate, body protein is nevertheless the body's largest potential glucose supply. Glycogen stores are limited, and fat stores, except for the glycerol moiety of triglycerides, do not provide net synthesis of glucose. But, of course, when body protein is broken down for use as energy or for glucose production, functional units are being destroyed.

5.5 Nitrogen disposal

When amino acids are metabolized, the carbon skeletons can be oxidized ultimately to carbon dioxide and water, both of which are easily disposed of by the body. The ammonia formed from amino acid degradation, which is toxic and which cannot be further oxidized metabolically in higher animals, must also be removed. The means for disposal of nitrogen varies from species to species. The most direct route and energetically least costly is as ammonia. However, such a system requires a large volume of water to keep the ammonia concentration below toxic levels. Surrounded

by water, many fish excrete nitrogen as ammonia. The ammonia is diluted by the water and is utilized by micro-organisms and water plants to form new amino acids and proteins.

The excretion of water by land animals is of insufficient quantity to adequately dilute ammonia. Therefore, ammonia is detoxified and nitrogen excreted in mammalian systems by formation of urea, a nontoxic, water-soluble compound which is readily excreted by the kidney. Urea formation does cost energy; four high energy phosphate bonds are spent for each urea molecule formed from ammonia. But the energy expenditure insures protection from ammonia toxicity.

For egg-laying species (birds and reptiles) neither ammonia nor urea is a suitable elimination form for nitrogen, particularly during the embryonic stage. There is no way for the egg to excrete any end products which would accumulate, and either ammonia or urea would become so concentrated as to be toxic to the embryo. Birds and reptiles therefore form uric acid as the end product of amino acid metabolism. The uric acid has low solubility and can form crystals in a part of the egg and not be detrimental.

Man also excretes uric acid but as the end product of purine metabolism, not as the end product of amino acid metabolism. Most other animals degrade the uric acid from purine catabolism to allantoin before excretion.

5.6 Ammonia fixation and transamination

Pathways of synthesis of the non-essential amino acids show a network of interrelationships. Except for cysteine and tyrosine, all of the non-essential amino acids can be synthesized from a glycolytic or citric acid cycle intermediate. The required amino group can be attached to the carbon skeleton by transamination or by ammonia fixation.

The major mechanism of ammonia fixation

is by the glutamic dehydrogenase (GDH) reaction, a reversible reaction favoring the formation of glutamic acid from α-ketoglutarate and free ammonia. As glutamate is a major donor of amino groups in transamination, the GDH reaction is very important for the synthesis or interconversion of non-essential amino acids. It is also important in amino acid catabolism, liberating ammonia, which then can become incorporated into urea.

The transaminase aspartate amino transferase (glutamate + oxaloacetate $\leftrightarrow$ α-ketoglutarate + aspartate) is the most active transaminase in animal tissues. Its activity is high in all tissues in both cytoplasm and mitochondria. Not only is this enzymatic reaction responsible for aspartate synthesis, but it plays an important role in the transport of reducing equivalents between mitochondria and cytoplasm. When NADH is formed in the cytoplasm during glycolysis, it must be re-oxidized to NAD in order for glycolysis to continue. NADH however, cannot cross the mitochondrial membrane and therefore cannot be re-oxidized in the electron transport system. But other cytoplasmic reactions requiring NADH can re-oxidize the NADH to NAD while forming products which can traverse the mitochondrial membrane, thus transferring the 'reducing power' to the mitochondria. Inside the mitochondrion the product can be re-oxidized and then can return to the cytoplasm. One such system is the malate shuttle, involving aspartate amino transferase and malate dehydrogenase, which occur in both compartments [4]. See Fig. 5.2. Oxaloacetate is only very slowly permeable to the mitochondrial membrane; thus the need for aspartate amino transferase. This process can be reversed if there is a need to transfer reducing power from the mitochondria to the cytoplasm, such as when hydrogen is required for gluconeogenesis from pyruvate in liver.

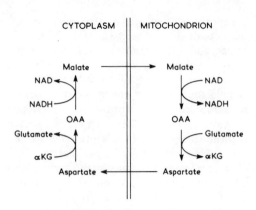

Fig. 5.2 Malate shuttle.

The transaminase alanine amino transferase (pyruvate + glutamate $\leftrightarrow$ alanine + α-ketoglutarate) is also very active. There appears to be an 'alanine cycle', which provides a means for carrying both nitrogen and carbon from muscle to liver [5]. During starvation, untreated diabetes, or cortisol treatment, when muscle protein is a major source of substrate for gluconeogenesis, the carbon skeletons of amino acids must be transported to liver, since muscle cannot synthesize glucose from them. Most of the amino acids are not released from muscle cells directly into the blood but are first converted to alanine. Alanine then reaches the liver where it can be rapidly converted to pyruvate by the highly active alanine amino transferase and is then available for glucose production [6]. As an added benefit, the nitrogen is also then present in the liver, the major organ of urea production.

Formation of glutamine (glutamate + NH_3 + ATP $\rightarrow$ gln + ADP + P_i) provides another nontoxic form for transporting nitrogen through the body. Highest in concentration of all circulating amino acids, glutamine can deliver ammonia to liver for urea production or to kidney for excretion as the NH_4^+ cation.

5.7 Amino acid metabolism and interconversion

A pair of amino acids whose metabolism is closely related is serine and glycine. Serine can be formed from the glycolytic intermediate 3-phosphoglyceric acid, requiring oxidation, transamination and dephosphorylation (Fig. 5.3). A transhydroxymethylation removes the hydroxyl group from serine to produce glycine. Thus, any metabolic problem in synthesizing serine might create a shortage of glycine, since the body's only other source of glycine would be dietary glycine and serine.

In addition to appearing in protein, serine and glycine have many other important roles. Serine, either as serine itself or after conversion to choline or ethanolamine, is a primary component of many phospholipids. Glycine is required for the synthesis of heme, which is contained not only in the hemoglobin in blood but in the cytochrome systems for oxidative phosphorylation. Glycine is needed also for purine synthesis and is one compound to which bile acids are conjugated before excretion by the liver into the intestine.

Glycine plays a special role in species that excrete uric acid as the end product of nitrogen metabolism. The formation of a uric acid molecule requires one glycine molecule. Since there are four nitrogen atoms per uric acid molecule and one nitrogen per glycine molecule, at least 25% of the nitrogen excreted must pass through glycine. However, in no protein, except those of silk and gelatin, do glycine and serine together account for as much as 25% of the amino acids. Therefore, the ability to synthesize serine and glycine is of great importance in these species. However, in the growing bird, for instance, the ability to synthesize these two amino acids cannot meet the demand. Thus glycine and/or serine is an essential amino acid for the growing bird. The fact that dietary glycine or serine can fulfill the requirement equally well [7] shows that it is the synthesis of serine from glycolytic intermediates rather than the conversion of serine to glycine that is limiting.

The two non-essential amino acids that require the presence and utilization of essential amino acids for their formation are, as we have said earlier, cysteine and tyrosine. Interestingly, the only part of cysteine that is truly donated by methionine is the sulfur group, the remainder coming from serine (see Fig. 5.4). Cysteine is used not only in protein synthesis but also forms taurine, to which bile acids are conjugated before excretion.

The sulfur-containing amino acids cysteine and methionine can have toxic effects if present in too great quantities [8]. Adenosyl methionine, an intermediate of methionine metabolism is thought to be a toxic factor. Increasing methyl acceptors such as serine and glycine in the diet decreases toxicity caused by excess methionine, suggesting that sufficiently rapid removal of the methyl group of

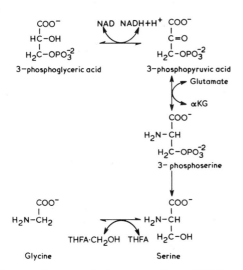

Fig. 5.3 Serine and glycine synthesis. THFA — tetrahydropholic acid.

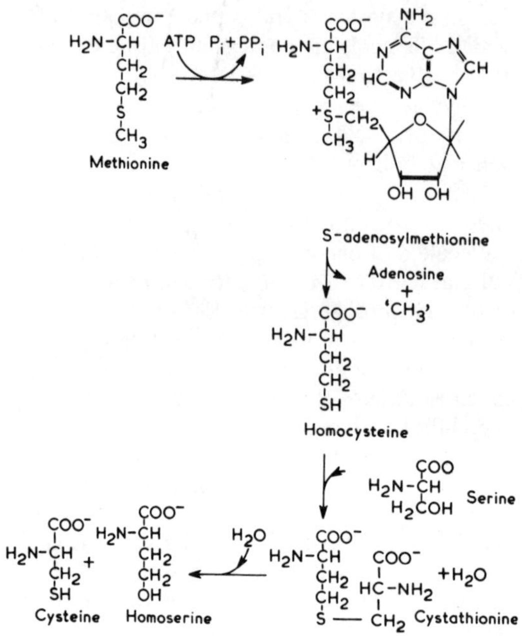

ATP P_i+PP$_i$

Methionine

S-adenosylmethionine

Adenosine +
'CH$_3$'

Homocysteine

Serine

Cysteine   Homoserine   Cystathionine

Fig. 5.4 Cysteine synthesis.

adenosyl methionine renders it less toxic [8]. The cause of cysteine toxicity is still unknown.

Tyrosine can be formed by the hydroxylation of phenylalanine. This occurs in liver and is catalyzed by the enzyme phenylalanine hydroxylase. The conversion of phenylalanine to tyrosine is obligatory in the catabolism of phenylalanine and is not required simply to maintain the level of tyrosine. In fact, tyrosine is as high as, or higher than, phenylalanine in most diets. Inability to convert phenylalanine to tyrosine due to an inborn defect in phenylalanine hydroxylase results in the disease phenylketonuria (PKU) [9]. PKU is signalled by the presence of phenylalanine and phenylpyruvate (a phenylketone) in the urine. Studies indicate that it is not a shortage of tyrosine but the excess of phenylalanine and its metabolites which is the deleterious factor, leading to severe mental retardation. Infants can be tested for PKU shortly after birth and if affected can be treated with a diet low in phenylalanine (not devoid, since phenylalanine is needed for protein synthesis). Adherence to the diet minimizes mental retardation.

Tyrosine has other roles and appears in other metabolic diseases. For example, it is the precursor of melanins, which form the body pigments. Albinism is the result of inability to convert tyrosine to melanin [10]. Inability to metabolize homogentisic acid, an intermediate of tyrosine catabolism, will result in the excretion of that compound in the urine, causing the urine to become dark. Known as alkaptonuria, this disease apparently has no detrimental consequences [11]. Tyrosine is also the major amino acid precursor of thyroxine and the catecholamines (epinephrine and norepinephrine).

Two other non-essential amino acids, proline and arginine, can be synthesized from glutamate semialdehyde (GSA), which is formed from glutamate by reduction with NADPH. Cyclization and reduction of GSA forms proline, whereas transamination of GSA forms ornithine, which can be converted to arginine in the urea cycle (Fig. 5.5). The reduction of glutamate to GSA appears to be a slow reaction but the oxidation of GSA to glutamate is fast. Consequently, it is difficult to form the semialdehyde fast enough to synthesize arginine and proline at a rate commensurate with maximal growth. Increasing the level of proline in a low arginine diet has been shown to increase growth rate, although proline has not been considered a growth promoting amino acid under any other condition [12]. There are two possible biochemical explanations for this. First, proline may cause a sparing effect, allowing most of the GSA formed to pass to ornithine and then to arginine rather than forming more proline. The other possibility is that during the metabolism

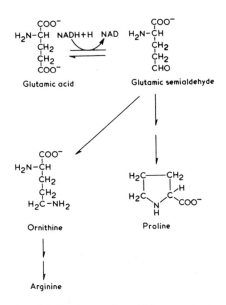

Fig. 5.5 Proline and ornithine synthesis.

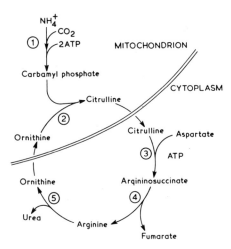

Fig. 5.6 Urea cycle. Enzymes: (1) carbamyl phosphate synthetase, (2) ornithine transcarbamylase, (3) argininosuccinate synthetase, (4) argininosuccinate lyase, (5) arginase.

of proline, glutamate semialdehyde is formed, increasing the concentration of GSA and thereby increasing the probability of transamination to form ornithine. The second explanation is consistent with studies using excess glutamate and proline [12].

Mammals do not require arginine in the diet for their survival. On the other hand, arginine is an essential amino acid for birds who have no urea cycle. Birds lack two enzymes to complete the urea cycle: the mitochondrial ammonia-dependent carbamylphosphate synthetase and ornithine transcarbamylase (see Fig. 5.6). Consequently in birds, formation or dietary provision of ornithine cannot yield arginine. Birds will grow well if citrulline is substituted for arginine but not if ornithine is given. Further studies have shown that in birds the major site for converting citrulline to arginine is the kidney and not the liver, the latter being the organ with the highest urea cycle activity in mammals. It has since been observed that mammalian kidney

has urea cycle activity. Furthermore, the ratio of activities of arginine synthetase and arginase in the kidney differ from that in the liver. In liver, arginase activity is very high while that of arginine synthetase is comparatively low. The ratio of arginase to arginine synthetase is much lower in kidney [13]. The liver is able to produce citrulline at a greater rate than it can produce arginine. Therefore, citrulline accumulates and can pass into the blood [14]. The arginine which is formed in the liver is rapidly cleaved to urea and ornithine [15]. The circulating citrulline can be absorbed by the kidney and converted to arginine, where arginase activity is not so high. Indeed, it has been shown with radioactively labelled citrulline in rats with ligated livers or kidneys, that the kidney is the primary site in mammals for synthesis of arginine for use by the body [16]. The brain also has the ability to remove citrulline from the blood and to synthesize arginine [16].

A possible advantage to the spatial separa-

45

tion of the roles of urea formation and arginine synthesis for body protein lies in regulation. Conceivably there could be a regulatory mechanism for arginine synthesis; when the body's need for arginine has been met, the synthetic machinery might be turned down. However, the function of detoxifying ammonia may continue to be needed. Thus, shutting down arginine formation in liver could result in ammonia toxicity.

Consistent with this hypothesis is the finding that, other than possibly with carbamylphosphate synthetase, there are no allosteric controls on enzymes of the urea cycle. The enzymes are effectively in fully active condition at all times. They do however, respond to the level of protein in the diet, but with chronic changes rather than with rapid allosteric changes. With higher dietary protein, urea production is increased, as would be expected due to the greater amount of nitrogen present. However, changing from a lower to a higher protein diet manifests the maximum rate of urea production within two days, whereas the urea cycle enzymes do not reach their maximum activities until five days later [17]. Therefore, it is apparent that the lower enzyme activity observed after two days was sufficient to produce urea at the maximum rate, and that the enzyme activities do not correlate well with urea production rates.

The amino acids whose syntheses have not been discussed here are essential amino acids, which must be provided by the diet.

All amino acids required for protein synthesis must be present simultaneously and in adequate quantities for protein synthesis to occur. All of the essential amino acids (with the possible exception of lysine, which is degraded very slowly) and adequate nitrogen must be included in a meal for protein synthesis to proceed normally. Receiving part of the amino acids in one meal and the remainder at a later meal is not adequate, since the body has no storage pool of amino acids and since most amino acids are degraded fairly rapidly [18]. A delay of 4 to 6 hours in supplementation of missing amino acids leads to detectable interference with protein synthesis. When the entire complement of amino acids is not present, the amino acids are degraded and used for energy or stored as glycogen or fat.

Following ingestion of a protein meal, there is a marked increase, particularly in liver, of the enzymes that catabolize amino acids. This assures that excess amino acids not used in protein synthesis will be degraded and that levels of circulating amino acids will not greatly increase [19].

Amino acid degrading enzymes become elevated also during starvation, when amino acids from body protein become the major source for glucose production. Several of the amino acid degrading enzymes release ammonia directly. This provides no threat of toxicity to the starving animal because substrate levels are low and the rate of ammonia release is slow enough so as not to overtax the urea production system. However, if a starving animal or person is fed a high protein meal, it can suffer digestive problems and ammonia toxicity. After World War II, there were several deaths due to ammonia toxicity when people from concentration camps were fed steak dinners. It appears that the best way to treat a starving individual is to feed a lower protein, high carbohydrate diet until the amino acid degrading enzymes are lowered and then to offer adequate protein diets to help replete body protein.

Though degrading enzymes are increased after protein ingestion, the higher priority of protein synthesis is insured by the K_m's of the two types of enzymes. Those enzymes which activate amino acids, readying them for protein synthesis, have K_m values near 10^{-2} or 10^{-3} mM. Amino acid degrading enzymes however have K_m's near 1 mM. Thus when amino acid levels are low, the activating enzymes will be operating nearer their maximum velocity than will the degrading enzymes.

5.8 D-amino acid metabolism

All amino acids used in protein synthesis must be in the L-form. Dietary protein from animal and plant sources provides only L-amino acids. But D-amino acids do enter the body, primarily from digestion of bacteria, whose cell walls contain D-amino acids. An enzyme, D-amino acid oxidase, existing primarily in kidney, converts D-amino acids to their α-keto derivatives. D-amino acid oxidase activity is normally at its maximum. In germ-free animals, which have no bacterial sources of D-amino acids, D-amino acid oxidase activity is comparatively low, but it can be induced to maximum activity by addition of quite small amounts of D-amino acids to the diet [20].

The use of D,L-amino acids in synthetic diets or in dietary supplements, is more economical since the D,L-form is less expensive to synthesize than is the pure L-form. However, the D,L-form does not substitute for the L-form equally well for all amino acids. For certain amino acids such as phenylalanine or methionine, the D-form is as well utilized as the L-form, whereas the D-forms of branch chain amino acids are not as well utilized as the L-forms. Examination of the metabolism of these amino acids makes the reasons for this phenomenon apparent. The first step in the metabolism of the L-form of the branch chain amino acids is transamination, forming the α-keto derivative. The α-keto acid can then be decarboxylated and further metabolized or can be transaminated back to the amino acid. The D-form of the branch chain amino acids will also appear as the α-keto derivatives and thence are indistinguishable from those α-keto acids derived from the L-amino acids. However, those α-keto acids which are then

decarboxylated will never appear as the L-form of the amino acid and will therefore not be available for protein synthesis. In other words, when the amino acid must pass through the α-keto derivative, it is subject to action from two competing pathways; the one taking it to the L-form and then to protein, and the other to decarboxylation and further degradation. The rates of these two activities determines how much of the D-amino acid will necessarily be removed from potential protein synthesis. In the cases of L-phenylalanine and L-methionine however, the first metabolic step is not transamination, the α-keto derivative is not an intermediate, and there is no pathway for catabolism of the α-keto derivative other than transamination. Therefore, the α-keto acids arising from the action of D-amino acid oxidase on D-phenylalanine and D-methionine must be transaminated to the L-amino acid before they can be further metabolized. Thus, D-phenylalanine and D-methionine must appear at some time as their L-forms and consequently will be available for protein synthesis.

References

[1] Neame, K. D. and Wiseman, G. (1957), *J. Physiol.*, **135**, 442–450.

[2] Unna, K. and Howe, E. E. (1965), *Fed. Proc.*, **4**, 138.

[3] Rose, W. C., Oesterling, M. J. and Womack, M. (1948), *J. biol. Chem.*, **176**, 753.

[4] Lardy, H. A., Paethau, V. and Walter, P. (1956), *Proc. natn. Acad. Sci.* (USA), **53**, 1410.

[5] Felig, P., Owen, O. E., Wahren, J. and Cahill, G. F. Jr. (1969), *J. Clin. Invest.*, **48**, 584.

[6] Ross, B. D., Hems, R. and Krebs, H. A. (1967), *Biochem. J.*, **102**, 942.

[7] Akrabawi, S. S. and Kratzer, F. H. (1968), *J. Nutr.*, **95**, 41.

[8] Benevenga, N. J. and Harper, A. E. (1970), *J. Nutr.,* **100**, 1205.

[9] Knox, W. E. (1972), In *The Metabolic Basis of Inherited Disease,* (eds) Stanbury, J. B., Wyngaarden, J. B. and Fredrickson, D. S., 3rd edit., p. 266. McGraw-Hill, New York.

[10] Fitzpatrick, T. B. and Quevedo, W. C. Jr., *ibid,* p. 338.

[11] LaDu, B. N., *ibid,* p.308.

[12] Rogers, Q. R., Chen, M.-Y. and Harper, A. E. (1970), *Proc. Soc. Exper. Biol. and Med.,* **134**, 517.

[13] Szepesi, B., Avery, E. H. and Freedland, R. A. (1970), *Am. J. Physiol.,* **219**, 1627.

[14] Drotman, R. B. and Freedland, R. A. (1972), *Am. J. Physiol.,* **222**, 973.

[15] Briggs, S. and Freedland, R. A. (1975), *J. Nutr.,* **105**, 1215.

[16] Featherston, W. R., Rogers, Q. R. and Freedland, R. A. (1973), *Am. J. Physiol.,* **224**, 127.

[17] Schimke, R. T. (1962), *J. biol. Chem.,* **237**, 459; and Marliss, E., Aoki, T. T., Felig, P., Pozefsky, T. and Cahill, G. F. Jr. (1970), In *Advances in Enzyme Regulation,* (ed.) G. Weber, **8**, 3.

[18] Geiger, E. (1947), *J. Nutr.,* **34**, 97.

[19] Watanabe, M., Potter, V. R. and Pitot, H. C. (1968), *J. Nutr.,* **95**, 207.

[20] Lyle, L. R. and Jutila, J. W. (1968), *J. Bact.,* **96**, 606.

Recommended reading

Schepartz, B. (1973), *Regulation of Amino Acid Metabolism in Mammals,* W. B. Saunders Co., Philadelphia, Penn.

Rose, W. C. (1938), The nutritive significance of the amino acids. *Physiol. Rev.,* **18**, 109–136.

Harper, A. E. Benevenga, N. J. and Wohlheuter, R. M. (1970), Effects of ingestion of disproportionate amounts of amino acids. *Physiol. Rev.,* **50**, 428–558.

Baldwin, E. (1963), *Dynamic aspects of biochemistry.* University Press, Cambridge.

Any general text on nutrition.

6 Vitamins

Animals fed purified diets containing exclusively carbohydrates, protein, and fats cannot survive. Vitamins and certain minerals must be included in the diet to sustain life.

Vitamins have little chemical resemblance to one another but are grouped together because of being essential dietary components with a similar general function. For convenience, vitamins are classed according to whether they are fat soluble or water soluble. With regard to the fat soluble vitamins (A, D, E, and K) some specific roles are recognized but other roles remain elusive. The water soluble vitamins (the B vitamins and vitamin C), however, all function as cofactors in metabolic transformations.

In many cases, clinical symptoms resulting from deficiency of a particular vitamin are not specific. That is, the same symptoms may arise from many other causes. There are numerous examples of syndromes that occur in many species (e.g. dermatitis, muscular dystrophy, infertility, gray hair) which may be curable by vitamin repletion in one species but are completely unresponsive to vitamin treatment in another. Furthermore, though the biochemical changes resulting from a vitamin deficiency are often predictable from the biochemical function of the vitamin, the outwardly displayed symptoms may or may not show an apparent relationship to the affected metabolic reactions. Many deficiencies are manifested in a general inadequacy for performing metabolism, with resulting secondary blockages in many pathways. Hence, the displayed symptoms may correlate poorly with specific biochemical functions. In this chapter we wish to describe some of the known roles of the vitamins and to distinguish those cases for which specific deficiency symptoms are currently explicable by biochemical function and those for which they are not.

6.1 Vitamin A

Vitamin A, a fat-soluble vitamin, occurs primarily as an alcohol and only in animal tissues. However, plants contain compounds called carotenes which can upon ingestion be converted by the intestine to vitamin A. Vitamin A plays a role in maintenance of epithelial structures, but its mechanism in this function is not well understood.

Quite well understood, however, is vitamin A's role in vision. The aldehyde derivative of vitamin A, retinal, in the active form has a *cis*-double bond at position 11. This 11-*cis*-retinal combines with the protein opsin to form rhodopsin, or visual purple. When light impinges on rhodopsin in the rods of the eye, the *cis* double bond is converted to the *trans*-form. The resulting change in conformation leads to the dissociation of retinal from opsin, and the stimulation of nerve endings, which is perceived as light. For the continuation of light perception, retinal must enzymatically be converted back to the *cis*-form and recombined with opsin. A deficiency of vitamin A can lead to an insufficiency in the amount of retinal that can cycle, causing night blindness. (Rods are concerned with vision in dim light.)

Vitamin A acid can overcome growth retardation and epithelial lesions due to vitamin A deficiency. However, the acid form does not overcome night blindness. This suggests that vitamin A acid is not readily reduced to the alcohol or aldehyde.

6.2 Thiamine (vitamin B_1)

The active form of thiamine in tissues is thiamine-pyrophosphate. It functions as a coenzyme in decarboxylation of α-keto acids (e.g. pyruvate and α-ketoglutarate) and in transketolation (in HMP pathway). In thiamine deficiency, blood levels of pyruvate and lactic acid are elevated. This result is explained by thiamine's involvement in the decarboxylation of pyruvate to acetyl CoA. Since tissues need energy and energy production from the citric acid cycle is reduced (lowered αKG dehydrogenase and pyruvate dehydrogenase (PDH) activities), the tissues must obtain greater amounts of energy from glycolysis. The greater flux and the inhibition of PDH result in an increase in concentration of pyruvate and lactate.

The classical thiamine deficiency syndrome, beriberi, is characterized by degenerative changes in the nervous system which develop in peripheral neuritis. The central nervous system is dependent on oxidative metabolism, particularly the citric acid cycle. Therefore, it is not surprising that thiamine deficiency should reveal itself with neural symptoms.

6.3 Riboflavin (vitamin B_2)

Mammalian tissues contain several flavoprotein enzyme systems, composed of a riboflavin-containing coenzyme and a specific protein. The coenzymes, flavin mononucleotide (FMN) and flavin adenine dinucleotide (FAD), are involved in dehydrogenation and hydrogen transport.

Symptoms of riboflavin deficiency include mainly dermatitis and impaired healing of skin lesions. The relationship of the symptoms to biochemical function is not obvious.

6.4 Pyridoxine (vitamin B_6)

Vitamin B_6 can occur as pyridoxine, pyridoxal, pyridoxamine, and pyridoxal phosphate. Pyridoxal phosphate is an essential co-factor for many amino acid metabolizing systems, including transaminases, decarboxylases, and dehydratases. Many of the neurotransmitters or inhibitors of neurotransmitters are formed by decarboxylation of amino acid derivatives. Examples include serotonin from 5-hydroxy tryptophan, γ-aminobutyric acid (GABA) from glutamic acid, epinephrine and norepinephrine from dopamine (a derivative of tyrosine or phenylalanine), and histamine from histidine. Because of its close involvement with neural transmitters, it is not surprising to find that vitamin B_6 deficiency results in disorders of the central nervous system. In humans, weakness, nervousness, irritability, insomnia, and difficulty in walking can accompany vitamin B_6 deficiency. Though these symptoms and others involving forms of dermatitis are not unique to vitamin B_6 deficiency, deficiency of this vitamin can be detected by a tryptophan-loading test. If vitamin B_6 is inadequate, the metabolism of tryptophan is impaired and intermediates of tryptophan metabolism, primarily kynurenine, are excreted in large quantities in the urine.

6.5 Niacin (nicotinic acid)

Nicotinamide, a derivative of niacin, is a component of the coenzymes nicotinamide adenine dinucleotide (NAD) and nicotinamide adenine dinucleotide phosphate (NADP). NAD and NADP are important in oxidation-reduction reactions, particularly in the transfer of hydrogens to or from aldehydes, alcohols, and organic acids. In this capacity, NAD and NADP are necessary for complete oxidative catabolism of carbohydrates, proteins and lipids. NADP in its reduced form (NADPH) is also necessary for the biosynthesis of fatty acids.

Deficiency of niacin creates a general inadequacy for performing metabolism. Symptoms of deficiency vary greatly from one species to another–black-tongue in dogs, pellagra in humans–and cannot currently be explained by failure of any specific biochemical reactions.

6.6 Pantothenic acid

As a component of coenzyme A, pantothenic acid is important in the disposition of two-carbon units. Coenzyme A can accept acetyl radicals (thereby forming acetyl coenzyme A) from pyruvate, citrate, and fatty acids and can then transfer them elsewhere. Acetyl CoA can transfer its acetate radical to oxaloacetate to form citrate, to choline to form acetyl choline (a neural transmitter), and to acetoacetyl CoA to form hydroxymethylglutaryl-CoA, a precursor of both ketone bodies and cholesterol, to name a few. Thus, coenzyme A is important in oxidative catabolism and in biosynthesis.

Insufficiencies of pantothenic acid lead to a large variety of syndromes in different species that are not clearly explicable by its biochemical function.

6.7 Biotin

Biotin is a co-factor of enzymes which catalyze CO_2 fixation with a concomitant hydrolysis of ATP. Pyruvate carboxylase, which requires biotin, is important both for gluconeogenesis and for maintaining or increasing intermediate levels in the citric acid cycle. Acetyl CoA carboxylase, also a biotin enzyme, is required for fatty acid synthesis.

When biotin intake is insufficient, there is a decrease in amino acid incorporation into protein, probably due to a reduction in synthesis of dicarboxylic acids. Biotin deficiency has also been shown to impair glucose utilization and fatty acid synthesis. Clinical symptoms, including dermatitis, depression, and eventually anorexia and anaemia, are not unique to biotin deficiency and are not obviously related to the biochemical function of the vitamin.

6.8 Folic acid (folacin)

As tetrahydrofolic acid (THFA), this vitamin participates in transfers of single carbon units. Formyl, hydroxymethyl, methyl, methenyl, methylene, and formimino groups are transferred enzymatically to THFA and from THFA to other compounds. These reactions permit the conversions of serine to glycine, homocysteine to methionine, and dUMP to dTMP.

The primary symptom of folate deficiency is megaloblastic anemia. A cell system which continually needs replacement, the red blood cells are among the first to manifest the detrimental effects of impaired thymidine formation.

6.9 Vitamin B_{12}

This cobalt-containing vitamin functions as a coenzyme in reactions involving intermolecular rearrangements (isomerizations) and reductions, primarily of single carbon groups and perhaps of sulfhydryl (SH) groups. For example, vitamin B_{12} is a coenzyme for the isomerase which converts methyl malonyl CoA to succinyl CoA. Vitamin B_{12} is also involved in the reduction of single carbon groups carried by THFA.

For absorption of vitamin B_{12} from the gut, intrinsic factor, a product of the gastric mucosa, must be present in the gut and available to combine with vitamin B_{12}. In the absence of available intrinsic factor, vitamin B_{12} deficiency can occur. Deficiency is manifested as pernicious anaemia, characterized by megaloblastic anaemia and neural lesions. The similarity of this hematopoietic problem to that seen in folic acid deficiency may be due in fact to a secondary deficiency of folic acid, since vitamin B_{12} is needed for reduction of some forms of THFA. Supporting this theory is the observation that the anaemia of pernicious anemia, though not the neural lesions, can be temporarily overcome by administration of folic acid.

6.10 Ascorbic Acid (vitamin C)

Ascorbic acid is a water-soluble antioxidant. Metabolically, it is involved in some hydroxylation reactions, such as the formation of hydroxyproline from proline that is already linked in peptide bond. It is also important in the complete oxidation of the aromatic amino acids. Ascorbic acid is also involved in the formation of norepinephrine and in the reduction of iron.

Most animals can synthesize ascorbic acid from glucose, but when man and other primates and the guinea pig are deprived of dietary ascorbic acid, scurvy develops. Connective tissue, growing bones, teeth, and blood vessels are the main systems showing impaired development or degeneration in scurvy. Insufficient cross-linking in collagen due to decreased hydroxylation of proline can explain the problems with connective tissue and the slowness to heal which is commonly seen in scorbutics. However, the pathological developments in scurvy are numerous and various, and not readily explicable by current knowledge of the biochemical functions of ascorbic acid.

6.11 Calciferol (vitamin D)

Though the mechanisms of its action are not understood, vitamin D has long been recognized as having a role in calcium and phosphorous metabolism and bone formation. In its active form, 1,25-dihydroxy cholecalciferol, vitamin D increases the rate of reabsorption of phosphate by the renal tubules, increases the rate of calcium and phorphorous absorption from the intestine, and permits physiological concentrations of parathyroid hormone to mobilize calcium and phosphate from bone.

Deficiency of vitamin D in growing animals causes rickets, an abnormal process of bone formation in which ossification is retarded. In adults, deficiency of both vitamin D and calcium can cause osteomalacia.

Vitamin D, a fat soluble vitamin, can be synthesized in the skin from a cholesterol derivative when it is exposed to ultraviolet radiation. Hence, vitamin D could be regarded as a hormone rather than a vitamin.

6.12 Vitamin E (tocopherol)

Since the tocopherols are fat-soluble antioxidants, a theory has developed that vitamin E's role *in vivo* is as an antioxidant. There is considerable evidence supporting this viewpoint but also many observations that are not explicable by this theory. There is currently no unifying theory of the biochemical functions of vitamin E.

Vitamin E deficiency can produce a variety of pathologies, varying according to species, age, and other dietary constituents. Infertility in rats, muscular dystrophy in many species (but not in humans), and pigmentation of muscle tissue in non-herbivorous animals are but a few of the observed manifestations of vitamin E deficiency. The great variability of symptoms complicates the task of determining the exact biochemical roles of the vitamin.

6.13 Vitamin K

Vitamin K is necessary for the formation of prothrombin in liver and thus plays an important role in blood coagulation. Deficiency of vitamin K results in prolonged clotting time and the possibility of severe hemorrhages. When adequacy of the prothrombin level is critical, as before surgery or delivery, vitamin K may be administered therapeutically.

Antimetabolites of vitamin K, such as dicumerol and warfarin, are used in moderate doses to treat conditions in which blood clots, i.e. blockage of capillaries, pose a threat. Excesses of these antimetabolites, particularly warfarin, are used as rodent poisons. Consumption leads to internal hemorrhaging when small vessels rupture. The lowered level of circulating fluid causes thirst and the rodent dies near a water supply, preferably outdoors.

Recommended reading

West, E.S., Todd, W.R., Mason, H.S. and Van Bruggen, J.T. (1966), In *Textbook of Biochemistry,* pp. 732–848, Macmillan Co., New York.

Wohl, M.G. and Goodhart, R.S. (1968), In *Modern Nutrition in Health and Disease,* pp. 213–322, Lea & Febiger, Philadelphia.

7 Diet and hormone interactions

From the previous chapters, it should now be evident that fluxes through the various metabolic pathways within cells are determined by the intracellular environments and that these environments are greatly affected by the amounts and types of nutrients ingested. Metabolites arising more or less directly from the diet have been shown to alter fluxes by increasing substrate concentrations and by inhibiting or activating enzymes. Several examples have also been given of hormones performing similar functions. Because diet composition and hormones can influence metabolism in similar ways, it is necessary to be aware of the interrelationships of these two factors in order properly to plan experiments and to interpret results.

Some of the interdependencies between diet and hormones are quite obvious. For instance, in the prolonged absence of dietary iodine, thyroxine cannot be synthesized, resulting in the disappearance of its stimulatory effect on metabolic rate. Or, if dietary protein is limiting or absent, hormones which are proteins or are otherwise derived from amino acids will diminish. Other interdependencies are more subtle, however. For example, a particular dietary factor may cause the release of a hormone, as when a high carbohydrate intake stimulates the release of insulin from the pancreas: or, a hormone may have a permissive effect on a nutritionally induced change. An example of this interaction occurs with high carbohydrate diets and thyroxine. An increase in malic enzyme activity results after long-term

ingestion of a high carbohydrate diet in a normal rat. A thyroidectomized rat however, exhibits no increase in malic enzyme with consumption of a high carbohydrate diet [1]. This shows that the presence of thyroxine is necessary for the manifestation of the nutritional effect. In still another type of response, a hormone present in large quantity may mask a nutritional effect. For instance, when thyroxine is present in excess, the normal increase in G6PD activity occurring with a high fructose diet is not seen because G6PD activity is already elevated maximally due to the high thyroxine [1].

The enzyme response obtained with various dietary treatments may well depend on the hormonal state of an animal, and likewise, a response to hormone administration may depend on the nutritional status. To illustrate this point, consider the enzyme changes following consumption of a high protein diet and those following glucocorticoid (e.g. cortisol) administration. With both treatments there is an increase in liver in activity of the transaminases, of gluconeogenic enzymes (G6Pase, FDPase, PEPcarboxykinase), and of several of the amino acid degrading enzymes (serine dehydratase, tryptophan pyrrolase, histidase). Since glucocorticoids cause increased rates of catabolism of body protein, the question arises as to whether the alteration in liver enzymes is due to the flood of amino acids entering the liver with either treatment or whether the high protein diet causes a glucocorticoid release and the glucocorticoid is directly responsible for the enzyme changes. To answer one of these questions, experiments were performed to compare the enzyme responses of adrenalecto-mized rats and intact rats to a high protein diet [2]. There were several possible outcomes. If there were no difference in response between the intact and the operated rats, one would conclude that neither the presence of the hormone nor its increased production is necessary for the manifestation of the high protein effects. On the other hand, if there were no change or less change in those animals lacking adrenal function, one would conclude either that the hormone is required for per-missive action or that increased output of the hormone is required for the metabolic changes. The latter two possibilities could be distinguish-ed by administration of replacement (not excess) doses of the hormone. The disappear-ance of any difference between the groups would indicate that the presence of the hor-mone is necessary but the increased production is not. The experiments showed, in fact, that most of the changes in enzyme activity that were observed in the intact animals were observed also in the animals lacking adrenal glands. Thus, it appears that the change in enzyme activities after consumption of a high protein diet is more related to the great influx of amino acids than to an increased secretion of a glucocorticoid. Furthermore, none of the adrenal hormones played a permissive role in these changes.

After adrenalectomy, the basal level of enzyme activity is lower than that observed in the intact animal. This suggests that these endocrine glands do play some role in main-taining normal levels of activity of enzymes associated with amino acid metabolism [2, 3]. It also creates a problem in interpretation of data. Should increases in activity following a treatment (feeding of a high protein diet, for instance) be compared as absolute increases or as percentage increases? The enzyme activities discussed here have been shown by antibody studies to be increased as a result of the presence of greater numbers of enzyme molecules, rather than through conversion from an inactive to an active form [4, 5, 6]. Therefore, either the synthesis rate of the enzyme has increased or the degradation has decreased, or both. An increase in the rate of synthesis (e.g. a doubling or tripling) at two different basal levels will cause the same proportional increase in enzyme activity but not the same absolute increase in activity. In the same way, a given decrease in degradation rate will produce the same pro-portional increase in enzyme activity but not the same absolute change. Thus, it is the pro-portional changes rather than the absolute changes which must be compared when looking for similarity or difference in responses [7].

If administration of a hormone causes parti-cular enzymatic changes and dietary manipula-tion causes similar changes, the two treatments when applied together can show a variety of effects. First, together the effect may be no greater than when the hormone treatment alone is applied. This would imply that a self-limiting maximum in enzyme activity has been reached. Second, the effects of the two treatments may be additive. This would suggest that no maxi-mum had been reached by either treatment. It would also suggest the independent action of the two treatments. Third, the two treatments may operate synergistically. That is, their combined effect is greater than the sum of their separate effects. And last, their effects together may be greater than one separately but less than the sum of the separate effects. This suggests either an overlapping of action or the attain-ment of a self-limiting maximum of activity before additive results could be seen. The high protein diet and cortisol interaction is an example of overlapping actions. The high pro-tein diet can produce increases in amino acid metabolizing enzymes in the absence of gluco-corticoid, and glucocorticoid can cause changes

Table 7.1 Effect of dietary protein content on the response of several liver enzymes to cortisol administration

Enzyme	Protein content of the diet			
	0%	8%	25%	90%
Serine dehydratase	1.7*	3.5	3.5	1.8
Glutamic-pyruvic transaminase	13.1	13.6	3.2	1.3
Glutamic-oxaloacetic transaminase	3.5	3.2	3.2	1.6
Tyrosine transaminase	4.7	1.5	1.7	1.2
Malic dehydrogenase	3.8	2.6	1.3	1.7
Sorbitol dehydrogenase	1.6	1.1	0.9	0.8

*All values are reported as $\dfrac{\text{activity after 5 days of cortisol}}{\text{activity without exogenous cortisol}}$.

(Data taken from [8]).

in these enzymes in the absence of dietary protein. The greatest relative response of certain enzymes to glucocorticoids occurs with a diet devoid of protein, whereas for other enzymes, some dietary protein is necessary to observe the maximal effects of glucocorticoids [1, 8] Table 7.1).

The major purpose of this chapter has been to show that enzyme responses to various dietary regimens may depend on hormonal status and that responses to hormone administration may depend on nutrient intake. Thus, in experiments using hormone alteration, it is important to specify clearly the details of diets consumed.

References

[1] Freedland, R. A., Murad, S. and Hurvitz, A. I. (1968), *Fed. Proc.* **27**, 1217.

[2] Freedland, R. A., Avery, E. H. and Taylor, A. R. (1968), *Can. J. Biochem.,* **46**, 1253.

[3] Harding, H. R., Rosen, F. and Nichol, C. A. (1961), *Am. J. Physiol.,* **201**, 271; and Willmer, J. S. (1960), *Can. J. Biochem. and Physiol.,* **38**, 1095.

[4] Segal, H. L., Rosso, R. G., Hopper, S. and Weber, M. M. (1962), *J. biol. Chem.,* **237**, PC3303.

[5] Schimke, R. T. (1964), *J. biol. Chem.,* **239**, 3808.

[6] Kenney, F. T. (1962), *J. biol. Chem.,* **237**, 1610.

[7] Szepesi, B. and Freedland, R. A. (1969), *Arch. Biochem. Biophys.,* **133**, 60.

[8] Hurvitz, A. I. and Freedland, R. A. (1968), *Arch. Biochem. Biophys.,* **127**, 548.

Recommended reading

Freedland, R. A. and Szepesi, B. (1971), Control of enzyme activity: nutritional factors. In *Enzyme Synthesis and Degradation in Mammalian Systems*, pp. 103–140. S. Karger, Basel.

8 Application of knowledge

The purpose of this chapter is to provide the reader with an opportunity to apply some of the biochemical and nutritional information presented in the preceding chapters. Due to limited space, the questions are few and arbitrary in nature and are not meant to be all-encompassing. The solutions require application of metabolic knowledge and principles. It is the hope of the authors that these exercises might serve as examples for an approach to future problem-solving.

Questions

(1) Considering that ammonia is normally a toxic substance, what is the advantage of continual production of ammonia from glutamate by glutamic dehydrogenase (GDH) in the liver? Further, what is the advantage of GDH being located exclusively in the mitochondria?

(2) Give a rationale for the fact that low protein diets can lead to 'fatty liver'.

(3) Glucose, glycerol, and fructose all are effective antiketogenic agents (i.e. they decrease the level of circulating ketone bodies, particularly when ketone bodies have been elevated above normal). Give a rationale as to how these agents manifest this effect.

(4) Why would glycogen be a much more efficient fuel for strenuous muscle activity than would blood glucose?

(5) It has been observed that after an overnight fast, if one were to drink 2 ounces of whiskey and shortly thereafter attempt to run a half mile, he would be unable to complete the task. Present a rationale for how ethanol metabolism could metabolically interfere with running.

Answers

(1) The advantage of continual production of ammonia from glutamate via GDH in the liver is to enable the animal to form urea. One of the two amino groups of urea must come from free ammonia via incorporation into carbamyl phosphate. One major source of this ammonia is glutamate, which can be formed by transamination of many amino acids with αKG. The value of transamination and of removal of nitrogen as urea is that it enables the animal to use the carbon skeletons of amino acids as a direct source of energy and for the formation of glucose. Inability to release ammonia from glutamate would result in difficulty in maintaining and regenerating αKG as amino acceptor and would thereby greatly curtail amino acid catabolism. The need for amino acid catabolism can be great under normal physiological conditions but is especially important during starvation, when amino acids from body protein are a main source of blood glucose. Without transamination and oxidative deamination, an animal would probably be unable to withstand even short (1 to 2 day) periods of starvation.

Even in animals that excrete ammonia as the endproduct of nitrogen metabolism, liberation of ammonia occurs primarily via GDH. Hence, regardless of the form of the endproduct of nitrogen metabolism, the functioning of GDH is of primary importance.

The advantage of GDH being located exclusively in mitochondria is related to the equilibrium of the GDH reaction and to other reactions which occur in mitochondria. The equilibrium of GDH strongly favors the formation of glutamate rather than of αKG, NADH, and NH_3. By being in the mitochondria where products of the reaction are continually being removed (αKG in the citric acid cycle, NADH in the electron transport system, and ammonia in carbamyl-phosphate formation), the reaction can occur in the direction opposite to that favoured by equilibrium. An additional advantage is the containment of ammonia, thereby limiting its access to blood and consequently to other tissues where it could be toxic.

There is also an advantage to carbamyl-phosphate synthesis occurring in the mitochondria. In mitochondria, all the substrates for the CPS reaction are readily available: ammonia from the GDH reaction, CO_2 from oxidative metabolism (i.e. citric acid cycle) and ATP from the electron transport system. The high concentration of reactants in the small space increases the probability of their combination with the enzyme.

(2) Low protein diets can lead to fatty livers for several reasons. Lipids, both those synthesized in the liver and those transported to the liver as chylomicra or NEFAs, require the formation of VLDL (very low density lipoproteins) or LDL (low density lipoprotiens) for transport out of the liver for storage in adipose tissue and use by muscle. These lipoproteins consist of triglycerides, phospholipids, some cholesterol, and an overcoat of protein. In protein deficiency, there may be inability to synthesize the protein coat for lipoprotein formation, and therefore transport of lipids from the liver may be curtailed.

The phospholipid fraction of the lipoproteins frequently contains many phospholipids with a lecithin moiety. Lecithin is synthesized from choline, which can be obtained from the diet or can be synthesized in the body from serine and methionine. Since serine is a nonessential amino acid, an animal's system can probably synthesize adequate amounts of it even when dietary protein is low. But methionine, an essential amino acid, may be insufficient in a low protein diet to support adequate choline synthesis. The resulting insufficiency of lecithin formation would decrease the availability of phospholipids for VLDL formation, thus preventing mobilization of fat out of the liver to peripheral tissues.

Even with a diet adequate in protein, if methionine and choline are both low, fatty liver can occur. Fatty liver due to a diet low in methionine and choline can be partially overcome by addition of choline for lecithin formation, but the condition will not be entirely corrected, since methionine for formation of the protein coat for the VLDL will still be insufficient. Supplementation of the diet with adequate methionine, even in the absence of choline, will completely correct the problem, as methionine is a precursor for both the protein coat and lecithin.

(3) Glucose, glycerol, and fructose all function as antiketogenic agents, but by several different mechanisms. Glucose manifests its antiketogenic properties primarily through effects on adipose tissue. Increased blood glucose causes insulin release, which 1) facilitates entry of glucose into adipose cells, thereby providing a source of α-glycerol phosphate (αGP) and 2) causes a decrease in activity of hormone-sensitive lipase (HSL). The increased αGP allows re-esterification of circulating NEFAs for storage in adipose tissue, and the diminished HSL activity decreases the release of NEFAs from adipose cells into the blood. Both effects result in lowered substrate avail-

ability in liver for ketone body formation.

The antiketogenic action of glycerol is directly within the liver. Glycerol cannot be phosphorylated in adipose tissue (prerequisite for esterification of triglycerides) but is readily phosphorylated in liver and can raise liver αGP levels as much as 5 times normal. This large increase in αGP tends to trap NEFAs as triglycerides or phospholipids, thus decreasing the concentration of activated fatty acids which could otherwise be converted to ketone bodies. The activation of fatty acids occurs in cytoplasm, where the activated fatty acid can combine with αGP, eventually to form a triglyceride or phospholipid, or with carnitine for transport to the mitochondria where ketone body formation takes place. The higher αGP concentration insures removal of a greater portion of the activated fatty acids as triglycerides and phospholipids, and leaves fewer available as precursors for ketone bodies.

Fructose acts as an antiketogenic agent through a combination of the mechanisms observed with glucose and glycerol. In liver, fructose can be converted to glucose, and in the process, concentration of triose phosphates, including αGP, are increased. Furthermore, fructose itself stimulates the release of insulin, although not as potently as does glucose. Nevertheless, the elevated insulin causes a decrease in HSL activity in adipose tissue and, along with the increased blood glucose, provides a source for αGP. The net effect is an increase in re-esterification of fatty acids in adipose and a decrease in availability of fatty acids for ketone body formation in liver.

(4) Glycogen is a more efficient fuel than glucose for strenuous muscle exercise for several reasons. First, availability of glucose from blood is not always dependable. Blood flow through exercising muscle is not continuous but intermittent, with small vessels continually closing and re-opening. In addition, the movement of glucose across the cell membrane is dependent in part on the presence of insulin, and during exercise, when there is increased circulating epinephrine, release of insulin is usually decreased.

Further, when glucose does enter muscle, it must be phosphorylated to glucose-6-phosphate (G6P), a step that is rather slow compared to the rest of glycolysis and one that is subject to severe regulation by its own product. G6P is usually high enough to cause significant (as high as 95%) inhibition of hexokinase. Thus, the flow through glycolysis beginning from blood glucose may be very limited in exercising muscle.

Muscle glycogen, on the other hand, can be mobilized and can pass down the glycolytic path without dependency on blood flow. High levels of G6P and F6P do not feed back as severely on glycogen breakdown as on hexokinase. The elevated F6P leads to functioning of the glycolytic path even with high ATP. Thus, energy can be generated anaerobically faster from muscle glycogen than from blood glucose.

Glycogen has a further advantage over glucose in terms of energy provided. The net yield of high energy phosphate bonds for each glucose molecule converted to lactic acid is two. With glycogen (except for those glucose moieties in a α-1,6 linkage), the yield is three high energy phosphate bonds. Thus, the energy yield is 50% greater when starting with glycogen

It should be pointed out that while muscle is at rest and is building glycogen, there is a cost of two high-energy phosphate bonds per glucose moiety stored. Hence, the overall net yield of energy in glycolysis from glycogen is less than from glucose. This is another example of a spending of extra energy by the body during times of plenty to make reserves for times of need.

(5) The difficulty in attempting any strenuous

exercise or long distance run after drinking strong alcoholic beverages following a period of fasting is related to production of lactic acid and to an impaired ability to reconvert that lactic acid back to glucose. Under normal conditions of exercise, there are two important energy sources available to muscle and to the central nervous system (CNS). These are muscle glycogen (primarily for muscle use) and blood glucose (heavily used by the CNS and somewhat by muscle, but not so efficiently as muscle glycogen). Working muscle produces considerable lactic acid, which is transported through the blood to the liver for reconversion to glucose (Cori cycle). The glucose can then be returned to the blood and used by CNS or muscle. During metabolism of high levels of alcohol, however, gluconeogenesis from lactic acid and from numerous other substrates is markedly inhibited and proceeds at a very reduced rate. Thus, there is accumulation of lactic acid, leading to muscle fatigue and to problems with acid-base balance and respiration. Eventually, there is a depletion of blood glucose. This is particularly true after a fast, since liver glycogen will be minimal and will not be a source of blood glucose.

Most alcohol metabolism occurs in the liver and results in the production of excessive amounts of NADH, leading to a great increase in the NADH/NAD ratio. Many studies show that the limited ability to metabolize alcohol is a result of inability to re-oxidize NADH in the cytoplasm. The high NADH/NAD ratio is further responsible for the impairment of two critical reactions of gluconeogenesis: 1) lactate → pyruvate, and 2) malate → oxaloacetate (OAA). Both reactions require NAD as cofactor. Impairment of the first reaction leads to a depletion of pyruvate, the essential substrate for pyruvate carboxylase, the first step in gluconeogenesis from compounds which

directly yield pyruvate, such as lactate, alanine, serine, etc. Thus, activity of the potentially rate-limiting enzyme of gluconeogenesis, pyruvate carboxylase, is markedly decreased primarily due to low availability of substrate.

In addition, when pyruvate is converted to OAA (in the mitochondria), it then leaves the mitochondria either as malate or aspartate and must be converted back to OAA in the cytoplasm to serve as substrate for conversion to PEP and back to glucose. A high NADH/NAD ratio in the cytoplasm slows the conversion of malate to OAA. Thus the efficiency of PEPcarboxykinase may be greatly reduced and the rate of gluconeogenesis markedly decreased due to inavailability of OAA.

Other reactions also compete for OAA, such as formation of malate (greatly increased with high NADH) and formation of aspartate. Aspartate formation may be stimulated by a chain of events which leads to increased glutamate concentrations. During alcohol metabolism, high concentrations of NADH may appear in mitochondria as a result of transfer from cytoplasm or from oxidation of acetaldehyde. High NADH can then cause accumulation of glutamate from the NAD-linked glutamate dehydrogenase reaction. High glutamate levels foster aspartate formation, thereby further limiting availability of OAA for PEP formation.

Thus, the high NADH/NAD ratio produced by alcohol metabolism decreases the rate of gluconeogenesis from lactate or pyruvate by affecting it at two steps, both NAD-linked oxidation-reduction reactions, and thereby leads to an increase in lactate which cannot be converted to glucose at a rate commensurate with its production. The net effect is lowered blood glucose, which would probably affect the CNS before muscle was severely affected, and high lactic acid, which could affect CNS and greatly increase muscle fatigue.

Index